What's Whole in Whole Language

Ken Goodman

RDR Books
Berkeley, California

What's Whole in Whole Language

RDR Books
2415 Woolsey
Berkeley, CA 94705
Phone: 510-595-0595
Fax: 510-528-0300
E-mail: read@rdrbooks.com
Website: www.rdrbooks.com

ISBN: 1-57143-119-5
Library of Congress Catalog Card Number 2005902658

Design and Production: Richard Harris
Proofreader: Diane Yeakey

Distributed in Canada by Starbooks Distribution,
100 Armstrong Way, Georgetown, ON L7G 5S4

Distributed in the United Kingdom and Europe by
Roundhouse publishing Ltd., Millstone, Limers Lane,
Northam, North Devon EX39 2RG, United Kingdom

14.95   Printed in Canada

CONTENTS

PREFACE

How whole is whole?

Some of the most effective whole language teachers aren't sure they are whole language teachers. Like all dedicated teachers, they're never quite satisfied with themselves. They continue to do things in their teaching that they think may be inconsistent with "pure" whole language theory. It is not the intention of this book to create a "wholier than thou" view of whole language teaching.

In indicating what's whole about whole language, the characterizations of whole language teachers and the criteria for whole language teaching are those of the author. Whole language is clearly a lot of things to a lot of people; it's not a dogma to be narrowly practiced. It's a way of bringing together a view of language, a view of learning, and a view of people, in particular two special groups of people: kids and teachers. Nothing in this book should discourage any teacher or group of teachers from developing their own version of whole language.

The book's major purpose is to describe the essence of the whole language movement — its basis, its features, and its future. More specifically it will:

• describe what we know about language and language development.
• present a whole language perspective on literacy development, both reading and writing.

- provide criteria that parents and teachers can use in helping children to develop literacy.
- mention examples of whole language programs that are already at work.
- suggest directions for building whole language programs and transforming existing programs into whole language programs.

More than anything else, a whole language program is an educational program conducted by whole language teachers. Perhaps this book will help them to recognize and define themselves.

WHOLE LANGUAGE: THE EASY WAY TO LANGUAGE DEVELOPMENT

This riddle has long troubled parents, teachers, and scholars: learning language sometimes seems ridiculously easy and sometimes impossibly hard. And the easy times are outside school, the hard times in school.

Virtually all human babies learn to speak their home language remarkably well in a very short time, without any formal teaching. But when they go to school, many appear to have difficulty, particularly with written language, even though they are instructed by diligent teachers using expensive and carefully developed materials.

We are beginning to work out this seeming paradox. Careful observation is helping us to understand better what makes language easy or hard to learn. Many school traditions seem to have actually hindered language development. In our zeal to make it easy, we've made it hard. How? Primarily by breaking whole (natural) language up into bite-size, but abstract little pieces. It seemed so logical to think that little children could best learn simple little things. We took apart the language and turned it into words, syllables, and isolated sounds. Unfortunately, we also postponed its natural purpose — the communication of meaning — and turned it into a set of abstractions, unrelated to the needs and experiences of the children we sought to help.

In homes, children learn oral language without having it broken into simple little bits and pieces. They are amazingly good at learning language when they need it to express themselves and understand others, as long as they are surrounded by people who are using language meaningfully and purposefully.

This is what many teachers are learning again from children: keep language whole and involve children in using it functionally and purposefully to meet their own needs. That simple, very basic discovery is leading to some dramatic, exciting changes in schools. Put aside the carefully sequenced basal readers, spelling programs, and handwriting kits. Let the readiness materials, the workbooks, and the ditto masters gather dust on the shelves — or better yet, donate them to community paper drives. Instead, invite pupils to use language. Get them to talk about things they need to understand. Show them it's all right to ask questions and listen to the answers, and then to react or ask more questions. Suggest that they write about what happens to them, so they can come to grips with their experiences and share them with others.

Encourage them to read for information, to cope with the print that surrounds them everywhere, to enjoy a good story.

This way, teachers can work with children in the natural direction of their growth. Language learning then becomes as easy in school as out. And it's more interesting, more stimulating, and more fun for the kids and their teachers. What happens in school supports and expands what happens outside of school. Whole language programs get it all together: the language, the culture, the community, the learner, and the teacher.

What makes language very easy or very hard to learn?

It's easy when:	It's hard when:
It's real and natural.	It's artificial.
It's whole.	It's broken into bits and pieces.
It's sensible.	It's nonsense.
It's interesting.	It's dull and uninteresting.
It's relevant.	It's irrelevant to the learner.
It belongs to the learner.	It belongs to somebody else.
It's part of a real event.	It's out of context.
It has social utility.	It has no social value.
It has purpose for the learner.	It has no discernible purpose.

The learner chooses to use it.	It's imposed by someone else.
It's accessible to the learner.	It's inaccessible.
The learner has power to use it.	The learner is powerless.

These lists show that a whole language program is more pleasant and more fun for both pupils and teachers. Is it also more effective? Yes, it is. With the language they've already learned, children bring to school their natural tendency to want to make sense of the world. When schools break language into bits and pieces, sense becomes nonsense, and it's always hard for kids to make sense out of nonsense. Each abstract bit and piece that is learned is soon forgotten as kids go on to further fractured fragments. In the end, they begin to think of school as a place where nothing ever seems to make sense.

That's why learning language in the real world is easy, and learning language in school should be easy, but is often hard.

What makes language learning hard?

A bottom-up view of learning
Moving from small to large units has an element of adult logic: wholes are composed of parts; learn the parts and you've learned the whole. But the psychology of learning teaches us that we learn from the whole to parts. That's why whole language teachers only deal with language parts — letters, sounds, phrases, sentences — in the context of whole real language.

Artificial skill sequences
Many so-called "skills" were arbitrarily chosen. Whatever research they're based on was done with rats and pigeons — or with children who were treated in the research like rats and pigeons. Rats are not kids; rats don't develop language or think human thoughts. Artificial skill sequences turn schools into mazes for children to stumble through.

Misplaced focus: language for itself
When the purpose of instruction is to teach language for its own sake, or to make kids discuss language like linguists, then the learner is distracted from what he or she is trying to say or understand through language.

Uninteresting, non-meaningful, irrelevant lesson
Uninteresting, irrelevant exercises are particularly tough on minority children who are constantly being reminded of the distance between their world and the school world. It's hard to motivate kids when the stuff they are asked to read and write, hear and say, has no relation to who they are, what they think, and what they do.

What makes language learning easy?

Relevance
Language should be whole, meaningful, and relevant to the learners.

Purpose
Pupils should use language for their own purposes. Outside school, language functions because users want to say or understand something. In whole language classrooms, the kids own their own language and teachers respect this ownership.

Meaning
Pupils should learn through language while they learn language. Language is learned best when the focus is not on the language but on the meaning being communicated. We learn through language at the same time that we're developing language. We don't learn to read by reading; we learn to read by reading signs, packages, stories, magazines, newspapers, TV guides, billboards.

Respect
Schools should build on the language development children have attained before they start school, and on the experiences they have outside school. Whole language programs respect the learners: who they are, where they come from, how they talk, what they read, and what experiences they already had before coming to school. That way there are no disadvantaged children as far as the school is concerned. There are only children who have unique backgrounds of language and experience, who have learned to learn from their own

experiences, and who will continue to do so if schools recognize who and where they are.

Power

School programs should be seen as part of the empowerment of children. Schools must face the bitter fact that children tend to become literate and succeed in school in proportion to the amount of power to use their literacy they and their families possess. Helping pupils become literate will not in itself give them power if society denies them power. But helping them to achieve a sense of control and ownership over their own use of language and learning in school, over their own reading, writing, speaking, listening, and thinking, will help to give them a sense of their potential power. Schools with effective whole language programs can help children to achieve power; they can provide real access to personally and socially useful knowledge through development of thought and language.

LANGUAGE: WHAT AND WHY?

What would we do without language? We'd still be smart, but terribly frustrated. Language enables us to share our experiences, learn from each other, plan together, and greatly enhance our intellect by linking our minds with others of our kind.

Many people think that if animals could talk — as in the Dr. Doolittle books — they would say intelligent things. Not so, for two reasons. Only humans are able to think symbolically — let systems of meaningless symbols represent our thoughts and through them our experiences, feelings, emotions, and needs. That's what makes human language possible. We also have an intense need for social interaction. That's what makes human language necessary.

Some animals have the ability to produce at least as varied a range of sounds as humans use in speech — mynah birds and parrots, for example. But their sounds lack the symbolic quality of language: they do not represent thought. If we could talk with them, we'd discover that they have nothing to say, that they lack what we have: intellectual capacity and the need for language.

What is language?

Sharing and growing

Language begins as a means of communication between members of the group. Through it, however, each developing child acquires the life view, the cultural perspective, the ways of meaning particular to its own culture. As children master a specific language, they also come to share a specific culture and its values. Language makes it possible to link minds in an incredibly subtle and complex manner.

Language is used to reflect on our own experience and to symbolically express it to ourselves. And through language, we share what we learn with other people. In this way, humanity learns what no one individual person could ever master. Society builds learning upon learning, through language. We even share our aesthetic and emotional responses to experiences. Narratives and poetry can so completely represent the experience of the writer that readers or listeners feel the same emotions, as if the actual experience were theirs. In fiction, language can actually create experience.

Written language greatly expands human memory by making it possible to store far more knowledge than any brain is capable of storing. Moreover, written language links us with people in faraway places and distant times, with dead authors. When written language could be cheaply reproduced and widely disseminated, information became a source of power. Limitations on literacy, or on its uses, became limitations on social and personal power.

Social and personal

Language is not a gift given to just a few people. Everyone possesses the gift of developing language, and many of us learn more than one, as the need arises in our lives. But this universality should not mask the unique achievement of each individual in language learning. As babies, we start with a capacity and a need to communicate with others, and we create language for ourselves. In doing that, each one of us moves toward the language of the home and community, but even so, each person's language retains personal characteristics. Each voice is recognizably different; each person's language has a distinctive style, as each person's thumbprint is not quite the same as anyone else's.

Language learning is often thought of as imitation. But people are more than parrots who produce sensible sounding nonsense. Human language represents what the language user is thinking, not simply what other people have said. How else could we express new ideas in response to new experiences? Human language makes it possible to express new ideas and be understood by other people who have never heard such ideas expressed before.

Yet if language were only our own, it would not serve our needs in communicating with others. We must come to share a language with our parents, our families, our neighbors, our people. Remarkably, the personal power to create language is shaped by the social need to understand others and to be understood by them, and the individual's language soon falls within the norms of the language(s) of the community.

Symbolic and systematic

Symbols have no meaning in themselves. "When I use a word," Humpty Dumpty said, in rather a scornful tone, "it means just what I choose it to mean — neither more nor less."

We can combine the symbols — sounds in oral language or letters in written language — into words and let them represent things, feelings, ideas. But what they mean is what we, individually and socially, have decided they will mean. The symbols must be accepted by others if the language is to work for us, but if we need to, we can stretch or modify them to mean new things. Societies and individuals are constantly adding, shifting, or modifying symbols to meet new needs and express new ideas.

But we need more than symbols. We need systems of organizing the symbols so that they represent not just things, feelings, and ideas but dynamic links: how events happen, why they happen, how they affect us, and so on. Language must have *system as* well as symbols, order and rules for producing it, so the same rules can be used for comprehending it.

Of course we can think of language as composed of sounds, letters, words, and sentences. But language cannot be used to communicate unless it is a systematic whole in the context of its use. Language must have symbols, system, and a context of usage.

Grammar is the system of language. It includes the limited number of rules necessary to produce an almost infinite number of utterances that will be understood by speakers of a specific language. Grammar provides word order and inflections (affixes for indicating person, number, tense). That's the most important thing a child learns before school. But the rules can't be learned imitatively since they are never visible in language. Rather, children infer them from experience. By learning to talk and understand speech, children demonstrate their remarkable ability to make these inferences.

Different and changing

There likely never was a human society without oral language. Prehistoric people, like the primary groups modern people belong to, required immediate, face-to-face communication, and oral language works well for that purpose. But language is not limited to speaking and hearing. We can use any symbol system to create language — or to represent it. Morse code was created to represent language for telegraph and radio use. Ships developed systems of signals using flashing lights or semaphore flags where distances were too great for voice communication. Tactile systems like Braille were developed to give blind people a means of access to print. And visual systems of hand signs were developed by and for deaf people deprived of access to aural communication.

It was not until societies required communication over time and space beyond the reach of the human voice that full forms of written language developed. People came to need to communicate with friends, family, or trade partners who did not live nearby. The culture became too complex for oral preservation and transmission. Written language was created to extend the social memory of the community and its communicative reach.

In the contemporary world, language even includes forms for communicating to and through computers and other machines. Whole language curricula accept the responsibility of the school to deal with the whole of language in this sense too.

But since individuals and communities are always changing, so language must change, always adapting to meet the personal and social needs of users. Just think about the following:

- The language of each generation is somewhat different from that of each prior generation. As we get older, we get "set in our ways." Young people are likely to question the *status quo,* and to adopt new language to represent changing lifestyles and life views.
- A certain portion of language comes into quick being among a particular group — musicians, teenagers, scientists, writers, activists — and achieves quick and widespread circulation. Slang appears and disappears. But not all of it is short-lived; sometimes a portion finds its way into more permanent language.
- Special forms of language develop among groups of people who share common interests and experiences: highly technical terminology and/or colorful metaphors. Doctors, lawyers, teachers, computer hackers, CB radio users, to name a few, develop a *jargon* understood only by the initiated. The British term is *registers,* special forms of language for use in special circumstances. We all have registers, in our jobs, our special interests, our religious and political activities.
- All languages are really families of dialects. People separated by distance, by physical barriers like rivers, mountains, or oceans, by social class, racial discrimination, or legal segregation develop variant forms of the language they share, differences in vocabulary, sounds, grammar, and idiom. Changes within each dialect reflect changes in the life experiences of each group and cause the dialects to drift apart, or at least to maintain their distance, even in an age of electronic communication.

Schools should welcome the dynamic, fluid nature of language. How marvelous the variety of language, dialects, and registers of pupils! How satisfying for teachers to support the full range of language development rather than confining it to arbitrary "proper" or "standard" language.

Why is language important?

Is language innate? Some scholars think so, especially when they look at how early and how well children learn it. But I think there's a much better explanation of why children achieve such universal precocious control of language.

Language for communication

Children are literally driven to learn language by their *need to communicate*. Sure, human beings are endowed with the ability to think symbolically. But actual language development is a matter of survival. At birth we are totally helpless. We depend for survival on our ability to get the attention of those around us.

People must also communicate to be fully functional human beings. Children have a great deal to learn as they develop, and almost none of it is a simple matter of maturation (though maturation is a factor in much of our learning). They must be in constant intimate communication with other human beings, and language is the key to communication. It is the means by which they come to share the sense that others have made of the world, as they seek to make sense of it for themselves. They learn language because they need it to survive. And they find it easy to learn because the purpose for learning it is clear to them.

Babies are aware of what language does before they are aware of how it does it. Even before they are aware of its communicative potential, they use it for social participation. People around them interact through language — well then, they will too. Very young children already vocalize when they hear other people talking. At six months or so, a child sitting in a high chair at the family dinner table will literally drown out other conversation with its own oral participation, a sure source of enjoyment and good feelings in most families. Often the first notable "words" are social signs like *bye-bye*. Such words don't communicate, but they establish an interpersonal function for language.

Soon children begin to have more explicitly communicative uses for language, to comment on the world or to express a need. Now their language grows rapidly to meet their new needs. They learn language as they use language to learn, and meanwhile they learn about language. From the beginning, all three kinds of language learning are simultaneous in the context of whole speech events.

Language for learning

Language becomes the medium of thought and of learning. In an important way, language development also enters the learning process directly. E.B. Smith suggests that cognitive development has three phases: perceiving, in which the child attends to particular aspects of experience; ideating, in which the child reflects on the experience; and presenting, in which the knowledge is expressed in some way. In this sense, it is not until an idea has been presented that learning is complete.

Language is the most common form of expression. From the earliest preschool learning and throughout life, it is important for people to have opportunities to present what they know, to share it through language, and in the course of this presentation, to complete the learning. This form of language development relates directly to ultimate success in school.

More than one language

Children born into bilingual or multilingual settings come to understand all the languages of their surroundings and to speak the ones they need to. Is it confusing for children to learn more than one language at the same time? No, not normally. They learn to speak to Grandma in her language, to the family in theirs, to the kids on the street in the language of the neighborhood. It has never surprised children in multilingual settings that there was more than one language spoken by the people around them. They simply sort out who speaks and understands what and when, and to whom to use which. Language is easy to learn when it's needed and available.

Many bilingual children fully comprehend a home language, but often respond in English in conversations. These children are showing their sensitivity to the subtle social values and complex functions of each language. They recognize that many of the people around them are bilingual, that each language tends to be used in particular situations by different family members and neighbors of different ages. They apply this sensitivity to meeting their own linguistic needs.

And please, do not believe that bilingual children are disadvantaged in some academic way. They are at a disadvantage only if their linguistic strengths are underappreciated and schools are failing to build on their strengths.

Bilingual children learn more than one language for the same reason that monolingual children learn only one: they learn what they need. That explains why foreign language programs in American schools have been so unsuccessful. The language is isolated from real speech and literacy events, and most American children have no use for the second language as they learn it. To be successful, school second language programs must incorporate authentic functional language opportunities. Canadian immersion schools, where French as a second language is also used as the language of instruction, clearly demonstrate the point.

LANGUAGE LEARNING:
HOW DOES IT HAPPEN?

Language is not innate, and not learned as imitation. Nor can human language be learned the way rats learn to run mazes in some simple stimulus-response manner. To control language, one must control the rules of language, and those must be invented and tried out by the learners.

Language learning is a process of social and personal invention. Each person invents language all over again in trying to communicate with the world. But these inventions involve the use of the surrounding public language, and they are constantly tested, modified, abandoned, or perfected in use against it. Parents and siblings do not really teach language. They help to shape its development by the way they respond. Fortunately for most babies, family members are so anxious to understand what the infant is saying that the earliest attempts at language are successful out of proportion to their merit. Anything vaguely close to recognizable language used in what appears to be an attempt to accomplish a linguistic function will tend to work. When it doesn't, the response may suggest another way to accomplish the goal, even if it's only vaguely understood.

All learning involves risk. Families tend to cherish first attempts at language and therefore diminish the risk to learners. They are free to fail and try again. Schools need to be equally encouraging of risk-taking in language development.

Halliday suggests that children often initiate language and parents follow along behind, tracking, responding, but letting the children set the pace and be in charge of their own development. There is so much language in the experience of young children, so much opportunity for testing out rules and hypotheses, using interchanges with others as resource material, that in due time control over the rules of the language is established, as well as over the sound system and the vocabulary. In the same way children gain control over the subtle pragmatic constraints on language, differentiating play from serious communication, becoming aware of who may say what to whom and when.

Function before form

Form follows function in language development, as in so many things. Children know what they want to do with language, and that stimulates their drive to control the form of language so that it meets their needs. It's worth repeating: language is easy to learn if it meets a functional need the child feels.

But here's where conventional wisdom gets in the way of understanding. Do you have to have control of sounds before you speak, of phonics before you read, of spelling before you write, of vocabulary before you use language? Not really. Children talk comprehensibly before they control many of the sounds of the adult dialect. They produce sentences long before they control the rules of sentence making. If they had to wait to control conventional spelling, they would never write, or even discover why spelling is important. Language use begins with a function and then involves experimenting with the language forms necessary to fulfill that function. Of course errors are made in the forms as they develop. We relish babies making them. But we become less tolerant of the miscues of older children, and somehow begin to think that development can go from stage to stage error-free. Whole language programs accept the reality of learning through risk-taking and error. Scribbling, reversed letters, invented spellings, creative punctuation, and reading and writing miscues are charming indications of growth toward control of the language processes. Kids are universally able to sort out language as they use it to meet their functional needs. If their language use in school is authentic, then they will not find it hard to get control of the language forms they need.

Whole to part

Baby books all have places to record a child's first word. But the idea that children begin with words and then put them together to make sentences is only an illusion. The illusion arises because physical control over the articulation of sound sequences is limited at first. But each *da-da* or *ma-ma* really is a whole utterance that means something like "Hey, come and get me. I want some attention." Children go through what some scholars have called a holophrastic stage. Each "word" is really an undifferentiated glob of language with a generalized meaning in certain situational contexts. As language develops, the glob begins to be differentiated into words and word parts. It takes on a grammatical structure, and at the same time moves toward more definite and specific meanings near to, but not necessarily the same as, the adult meanings. The child's "pick up" may mean both "pick me up" and "put me down."

Language is actually learned from whole to part. We first use whole utterances in familiar situations. Then later we see and develop parts, and begin to experiment with their relationship to each other and to the meaning of the whole. The whole is always more than the sum of the parts and the value of any part can only be learned within the whole utterance in a real speech event.

The rules for producing language utterances are induced from the early holophrastic units. "I taked it." "I pick-upped my toys." "He gots more." "Me wanna turn." So often the errors children make are the best indicators of their growth. When they start to generate their own rules and reveal them, we learn much about them, especially that they feel free to experiment and learn. Keeping children from making mistakes is a sure way to make them insecure and to inhibit their ultimate development.

But whether we're talking about learning to make sense of print as beginning readers, learning to read a TV guide, or learning to write a research report in a high school science class, the constituent parts or "skills" can't be learned outside of the whole experience at any stage of development. You can't learn to write a letter by first learning to write salutations and then opening paragraphs and then formal closings. None of these make any real sense outside a real situation in which a letter is the most useful way of meeting the need to communicate — to get information, to say thanks, to invite some real person to a real event. If we want to keep language learning easy, we have to help learners learn from whole to part.

Learning how to mean

Halliday explains the inseparable relationship between meaning and language development:

> The child is learning to be and to do, to act and to interact in meaningful ways. He is learning a system of meaningful behavior; in other words, he is learning a semiotic system. Part of his meaningful action is linguistic. But none of it takes place in isolation; it is always within some social context. So the content of the utterance is the meaning that it has with respect to a given function, to one or other of the things that the child is making language do for him. It is a semiotic act which is interpretable by reference to the total range of semiotic options, the total meaning potential that the child has accessible to him at that moment.

Schools frequently isolate language from its meaningful functional use. Then they change language into non-language. Only in the social context of language usage does it have a meaning potential for the learner, and only in such context is it language and easy to learn. From the very earliest beginnings, language is inseparably related in the child's mind to sensibility. If we turn it into nonsense, then it is not easy to learn but hard.

Speech and literacy events

Oral language occurs in speech events. A speech event includes not only the language text (the connected discourse itself) but also the people speaking and/or listening, their purposes, intentions, and social relationships. It includes the context of the situation — the physical setting, the cultural and social constraints, the emotions of the participants. The choice of register will depend on all these characteristics of the speech event. Participants in speech events know whether they have been successful in their intentions and modify their participation — including their language — to become more effective.

Written language occurs in literacy events. These have all the characteristics of speech events with one exception. In speech events, both speaker and listener are present, often switching roles. In most literacy events only the writer or the reader is present. The writer must have a *sense of* the audience, the reader a *sense* of the author. Though there is always a situational context of some sort, literacy events usually do not have the close relationship to a physical context that speech events do. So written texts must also include cues that provide those "senses."

More than once we have described how children develop their own language within speech events. They also begin to develop their competence with print in response to literacy events long before they go to school. At a very young age, children respond to books and to print in the environment and to adults reading to them. Optimal literacy development will occur in rich written (printed) language contexts.

Carol Edelsky says schools break the link between authentic language and natural speech and literacy events. They turn language into abstraction and essentially destroy it. This decontextualizing makes it hard to learn language. You will not be surprised to learn that a successful whole language program consists, to the fullest extent possible, of authentic speech and literacy events.

Two forces — outward and inward bound

Physicists talk about the centrifugal force, which causes something to move away from the center (as a ball on a string does when it's being whirled and the whirler lets go of the string), and about the opposing centripetal force (for example, gravity), which causes an object to seek the center. Placing a satellite in orbit is a matter of bringing these forces into balance.

Here is an apt metaphor for the forces shaping children's language.

The creative force inside them causes them to invent language and to constantly expand its limits and use. Outside them, the community pushes its language back toward the center of shared language and shared meaning. If the creative forces were unchecked, the individual's language would not work for social communication. But children's need to understand and be understood causes them to be sensitive to social response and to move toward the language norms of the social dialect. Again, it is only when children attempt purposeful use of language in real social contexts that these forces play against each other and shape language. Schools can support this process, but they can't short-circuit it by teaching the social norms in some prior, decontextualized way.

Language in school and out

A simple principle should now be clear. Language development is really the same in and out of school. Whatever makes language easy to learn outside of school will also make it easier to learn in school. And what makes it hard to learn is the same, in school or out. Successful school programs are based on an understanding of natural language development. The school facilitates language if the program involves authentic speech and literacy events, if the teacher is knowledgeable about language development and able to monitor and support its growth.

Of course there are unique language functions in school that relate to its own character as a community of learners, and to its focus on increasingly advanced and abstract areas of human knowledge. Schools have their unique speech and literacy events. Still, the basic principles of human language learning hold. Language development and learning through language will prosper when schools focus on what makes language easy to learn. This is a theme that will be pursued as we talk about a whole language curriculum in the next chapter.

Is written language different?

Oral and written language are two parallel language processes, different sets of language registers, which overlap to some extent. If you are literate, that means that sometimes writing is a better way of achieving a particular purpose, sometimes talking. You could write your sister who lives in another city, or telephone her. The latter method is more expensive, and doesn't leave a permanent record.

Written language has all the basic characteristics of oral language: symbols and system used in the context of meaningful language acts (literacy events). It is tempting (and people have done it) to treat written language not so much as language itself, but as a kind of coded representation of speech. This is unfortunate for a number of reasons. It leads us, in school, to expect reading and writing to be learned differently from speaking and listening, and to accept the belief that many children will have difficulty becoming literate.

Most people learn to talk before they learn to read and write, and it helps to do so. But hearing-impaired people can learn to read and write. And in learning second languages, many people have more need and opportunity to read than to speak. In this case, reading will often be the first of the four language processes to develop. Simply put, people will learn whatever language forms and processes they need the most.

Written language is not simply a way of recording oral language. For example, consider a simple chart, say a TV or a radio schedule in your newspaper. Because writing uses two-dimensional space, a lot of information can be presented in tabular form. Furthermore, a particular portion of the information can be accessed easily: what's on at 7 p.m., for example.

Functions of written language.
Written language has several important functions in a literate society:

- *Environmental print* provides information such as street names, addresses, store names, directions, and regulations (like Keep *off the Grass* or *Curb Your Dog*).
- *Occupational print* is the reading and writing that is part of doing one's job. School age children are students by occupation, but they also use written language as they play at adult occupations.
- *Informational print is* used to store, organize, and retrieve information. It can be very compact and dense, as in the case of phone books, or

attractively organized to highlight certain information, as in newspaper advertisements.

- *Recreational print* is the reading and writing we choose to do during our leisure time: fiction and non-fiction material related to hobbies and special interests.
- *Ritualistic print* is the written language many religions use in their rituals. Often texts are in an ancient language not well understood even by the participants.

Learning written language

Why do people create and learn written language? They need it! How do they learn it? *The* same way they learn oral language, by using it in authentic literacy events that meet their needs. Often children have trouble learning written language in school. It's not because it's harder than learning oral language, or learned differently. It's because we've made it hard by trying to make it easy. Frank Smith wrote an article called *"12 Easy Ways to Make Learning to Read Hard."* Every way was designed to make the task easy by breaking it up in small bits. But by isolating print from its functional use, by teaching skills out of context and focusing on written language as an end in itself, **we** made the task harder, impossible for some children. The one "hard" way Smith advocates is to find out what children are doing and to help them do it. What they are doing is trying to make sense of print. The way to help them do it is to make school a literate environment full of literacy events, with an insightful teacher present to monitor their development toward literacy and help it happen.

SCHOOL: A WHOLE LANGUAGE VIEW

These days many people are skeptical about positive, humanistic programs that do *not* depend heavily on technology. Technocrats think that education can be packaged in kits, workbooks, and mastery learning programs, and judged by pre-tests and post-tests. They think that whole language teachers don't know what they're doing or what kids are learning. Whole language teachers are accused of thinking they can make kids literate just by loving them.

Whole language teachers need not be defensive or apologetic. They believe in kids, respect them as learners, cherish them in all their diversity, and treat them with love and dignity. That's a lot better than regarding children as empty pots that need filling, as blobs of clay that need molding, or worse, as evil little troublemakers forever battling teachers. Whole language teachers believe that schools exist for kids, not that kids are to be filled and molded by behavior modification or assertive discipline into look-alike, act-alike, talk-alike Barbie and Ken dolls.

Whole language teachers believe there is something special about human learning and human language. They believe all children have language and the ability to learn language, and they reject negative, elitist, racist views of linguistic purity that would limit children to arbitrary "proper" language. Instead, they view their role as helping children to expand on the marvelous language they already use. They expect them to learn and they are there to help them do it.

Can school be fun? You bet! It not only can be, it should be. Learning in school should be as easy and as much fun as it is outside of school. What's more, if kids are enthusiastic and enjoy learning, then teaching is fun too! Whole language teachers admit they love teaching — and what's wrong with that, even if the pay isn't so great? Whole language teachers are proud professionals!

But there is more to whole language than this positive view of kids, a *whole* lot more, if you'll pardon the pun. Whole language teachers draw on scientific theories rooted soundly in research from linguistics, language development, socolinguistics, psycholinguistics, anthropology, and education as they build curriculum, plan instruction, evaluate progress. The humanistic and scientific bases of whole language teaching support each other. They make it possible for teachers to operate as effective, compassionate professionals with the type of confidence that's based on knowledge and commitment. In this chapter we'll explore this a bit further.

What is the basis of whole language teaching?

Whole language is firmly supported by four humanistic-scientific pillars. It has a strong theory of learning, a theory of language, a basic view of teaching and the role of teachers, and a language-centered view of curriculum.

A learning theory

Chapter two already spelled it out:

- Language learning is easy when it's whole, real, and relevant; when it makes sense and is functional; when it's encountered in the context of its use; when the learner chooses to use it.
- Language is both personal and social. It's driven from inside by the need to communicate and shaped from the outside toward the norms of the society. Kids are so good at learning language that they can even overcome counter-productive school programs.
- Language is learned as pupils learn through language and about lan-

guage, all simultaneously in the context of authentic speech and literacy events. There is no sequence of skills in language development. Teaching kids about language will not facilitate their use of language. The notion that "first you learn to read and then you read to learn" is wrong. Both happen at the same time and support each other.

- Language development is empowering: the learner "owns" the process, makes the decisions about when to use it, what for and with what results. Literacy is empowering too, if the learner is in control of what's done with it.

- Language learning is learning how to mean: how to make sense of the world in the context of how our parents, families, and cultures make sense of it. Cognitive and linguistic development are totally interdependent: thought depends on language and language depends on thought.

- In a word, language development is a holistic personal-social achievement.

A language theory

Whole language teaching is also based on scientific knowledge and theories about language. Halliday says we have treated language too solemnly but not seriously enough. We have tended to accept stuffy, narrow views of language. Language purists worry us about being totally proper in our language use, and they appoint themselves as judges. This uptight solemnity masks a total lack of respect for human language. It confuses the effectiveness of language with the status of the people who speak it. The language of people with power and social status is taken to be better than the language of people without it. Social attitudes toward language reflect social attitudes toward people.

Ours is a more serious and scientific view of language. Whole language teachers understand that there is no language without symbols and system. Every dialect of every language has register and grammar. People who speak differently are not deficient in any linguistic sense. Mark Twain, with a writer's insight, expressed this well in his explanatory note immediately preceding *Huckleberry Finn*:

In this book a number of dialects are used, to wit: the Missouri Negro dialect; the extremist form of the backwoods South-Western dialect; the ordinary Pike-County dialect; and four modified varieties of this last. The shadings have not been done in a haphazard fashion, or by guess-work; but painstakingly, and with the trustworthy guidance and support of personal familiarity with these several forms of speech.

I make this explanation for the reason that without it many readers would suppose these characters were trying to talk alike and not succeeding.

Whole language is whole. It does not exclude some languages, some dialects, or some registers because their speakers lack status in a particular society. Every language form constitutes a precious linguistic resource for its users. This does not mean that whole language teachers are not aware of the social values assigned to different language varieties and how these affect people who use them. But they can put these social values in proper perspective.

Language is inclusive, and it is indivisible. Whole language teaching recognizes that words, sounds, letters, phrases, clauses, sentences, and paragraphs are like the molecules, atoms, and subatomic particles of things. Their characteristics can be studied, but the whole is always more than the sum of the parts. If you reduce a wooden table to the elements which compose it, it's no longer a table. The characteristics of carbon, hydrogen, and some other bits may be studied and so help us understand how a table can be, but we don't build a table with them.

Language is language only when it's whole. Whole text, connected discourse in the context of some speech or literacy event, is really the minimal functional unit, the barest whole that makes sense. When teachers and pupils look at words, phrases, sentences, they do so always in the context of whole, real language texts that are part of real language experiences of children.

It had to come. Linguists and others are turning their attention from smaller bits and pieces to whole texts. They have begun to provide information on what makes a text a text and how people are able to produce comprehensible texts and make sense of them. Now we are beginning to realize that we've made mistakes in school when we tried to simplify language learning. Controlled vocabulary, phonic principles, or short, choppy sentences in primers and pre-primers produced non-texts. What we gave children didn't hang together, was unpredictable, and violated the expectations of even young readers who knew already how a real story works. Above it all hung the dark cloud of irrelevance and dullness. And we taught writing by drilling pupils on handwriting, spelling, and other mechanics, and so distracted them from what they already knew through oral language about producing whole functional texts.

Writing and reading are both dynamic, constructive processes. Writers must decide how much to provide so that readers will be able to infer and recreate what the writer created in the first place. Readers will bring to bear their knowledge of the text, their own values, their own experiences, as they make sense of a writer's text. Texts must be real, and not thrown together to fit some vocabulary list or phonics sequence. Writers must have a sense of audience, and readers must have a sense of the writer. Real writers have something to say, and real readers know how to understand and respond.

Whole language teachers have a basic sense of how language works. Lewis Carroll said, "Take care of the sense and the sounds will take care of themselves." Whole language teachers know, when they work with language that is whole and sensible, that all the parts will be in proper perspective and learning will be easy.

A view of teaching

Respect for and understanding of learning and language is matched by respect for and understanding of teaching.

Whole language teachers regard themselves as professionals. They draw constantly on a scientific body of knowledge in carrying out their work; they know about language, learning, kids, curriculum, and methodology. They take responsibility for their successes and failures. And they expect to be given the room to use their professional abilities and knowledge. They expect respect from their pupils, their administrators, and the public, and understand that respect must be earned by professional conduct. They take pride and pleasure in their work. They are confident in their teaching and in their decision-making because they are confident in the humanistic-scientific bases of their practice. They expect a degree of autonomy in their classrooms, for no professional can function if locked into rigid administratively imposed strictures — in their case, programs, curricula, and materials. They vary the use of adopted texts and prescribed curricula to meet the needs of their pupils in accordance with their best professional judgment. They apply criteria to methods, materials, and curricula and evaluate their potential effect on their pupils. In some circumstances they may find it necessary to reject certain materials and programs, just as a medical doctor reserves the professional right to reject certain treatments, drugs, and procedures.

Let's not beat around the bush. Basal readers, workbooks, skills sequences, and practice materials that fragment the process are unacceptable to whole language teachers. Their presentation of language phenomena is unscientific, and they steal teachers' and learners' time away from productive reading and writing. Many whole language teachers don't use basals at all, but build their programs around children's literature, often in thematic units. Some teachers salvage what they can — whatever good children's literature there is in their basals — to support the whole language program. But some programs — among them so-called mastery-learning programs — are so rigidly based on arbitrary skill drills and rigid pre-test, test, post-test sequences that the program is at odds with whole language criteria. Furthermore, rigid programs monopolize school time and turn progress into progress-through-the-program, rather than progress in real learning. Teachers are reduced to robots: technicians acting out someone else's script. In fact, such tightly controlled programs are often based on assumptions of teacher incompetence. Whole language teachers have the right and obligation to reject them, on behalf of the kids they teach and the professionalism they embody.

Whole language teachers understand that learning ultimately takes place one child at a time. They seek to create appropriate social settings and interactions, and to influence the rate and direction of personal learning. They are utterly convinced that teachers guide, support, monitor, encourage, and facilitate learning, but do not control it. They are aware of the universals of human learning, of language and cognitive processes, but they understand the different paths each learner must take. They expect and plan for growth and do not impose arbitrary standards of performance.

Whole language teachers are never completely satisfied. They keep trying to make the curriculum more relevant, to make language experiences in school as authentic and relevant as those outside school, to reach all children and help them expand their language competence as they continue to learn through language.

A view of curriculum

Integration

If language is learned best and easiest when it is whole and in natural context, then integration is a key principle for language development and learning through language. In fact, language development and content become a dual curriculum. For learners it's a single curriculum focusing on what is being learned, what language is being used for. But for teachers there is always a double agenda: to maximize opportunities for pupils to engage in authentic speech and literacy events while they study their community, do a literature unit on Lloyd Alexander, carry out a scientific study of mice, or develop a sense of fractions and decimals. The teacher evaluates both linguistic and cognitive development. Speaking, listening, writing, and reading are all happening in context of the exploration of the world of things, events, ideas, and experiences. The content curriculum draws on the interests and experiences children have outside of school, and thus incorporates the full range of oral and written language functions. It becomes a broad, rich curriculum that starts where learners are in language and knowledge and builds outward from there.

Individual growth, not achievement of absolute levels, is the goal. Whole language teachers accept pupil differences. They plan for expansion of effectiveness and efficiency in language, and expansion of knowledge and understanding of the world in each individual child.

Language processes are integrated as well. Children speak, listen, write, or read as they need to. If a puppet show is developed to dramatize a Lloyd Alexander story, then the story will be *read,* an outline or script will be *written,* and various class members will participate as *actors,* stage hands, or *audience.* If mice are studied, groups may *discuss* and plan their study, resource materials may be *read,* posters planned and *written,* observations made and *recorded, written* and *oral* reports made. Manipulatives in math may be used to explore fractions, findings *discussed,* and conclusions *written*-up. None of this is new, of course. But integration becomes the central motif in a whole language curriculum.

Choice, ownership, relevance

Authenticity is essential. Kids need to feel that what they are doing through language they have chosen to do because it is useful, or interesting, or fun for them. They need to own the processes they use: to feel that the activities are their own, not just school work or stuff to please the teacher. What they do ought to matter to them personally. Achieving the goal of providing for choice, ownership, and relevance throughout the curriculum is neither simple nor easy. But whole language teachers keep these goals in mind to ensure that the curriculum is most effective.

Language across the curriculum

In elementary classrooms with one teacher, this kind of curriculum is not hard to achieve. For departmentalized secondary schools the concept of *language across the curriculum* has spread from England to most other English-speaking countries. Content area teachers are urged to consider how language is used in their fields and then think of their curriculum as a dual curriculum with the double agenda it implies. Math teachers need to think of the language of math as a special register, and to help students learn to control it as they deal with math concepts and the solution of math problems. English teachers, librarians, and specialists in reading and writing need to plan with and even team-teach with content area teachers to achieve greater integration and greater authenticity.

Thematic units

Whole language teachers organize the whole of or a large part of the curriculum around topics or themes: *What are the risks of nuclear war? Is water pollution a danger in our community? The history of our neighborhood. How to take care of hamsters. Nutrition in mice.* They can be science units, social science units/literature units, or units that integrate all three, as well as the arts, humanities, and even physical education. A unit provides a focal point for inquiry, for use of language, for cognitive development. It involves pupils in planning, and gives them choices of authentic, relevant activities within productive studies.

What is a whole language classroom?

The splendid organization of whole language classrooms is not always apparent to a casual observer. The kids and teacher plan together what they will do, when they will do it and how, what materials will be needed, how they will be obtained or distributed, who will be where. Long-range plans provide a general framework, and short-range plans make details explicit. Just listen for the buzz of activity, see the level of participation of kids and teacher, enjoy the sense of well-being and ease everyone exhibits, admire the relatively smooth transitions, and relish the pervasive sense of order. The whole language teacher is clearly in charge, but it may take a visitor a few minutes to locate the busy adult doing many things in many parts of the room.

Clearly some classrooms lend themselves better physically to the range of activities that go on in a whole language classroom than others do. It doesn't help if there are rows of seats bolted to the floor. On the other hand, Lillian Weber has helped New York teachers to conduct open education by literally making use of the school corridors. The view of language, learning, teaching, and curriculum is what makes a whole language classroom; the physical environment can be adapted to fit.

A literate environment

In a whole language classroom, there are books, magazines, newspapers, directories, signs, packages, labels, posters, and every other kind of appropriate print all around. Pupils bring in all kinds of written language materials appropriate to their interests and the curriculum. Primary classrooms have mailboxes, writing centers complete with a wide range of paper and implements, a library comer, a newsstand, and appropriate labels for everything. No one is too young to participate in the creation of a literate environment: to dictate a story, label, put together the displays and bulletin boards, or simply experience how the literate environment is created.

Centers and resources

Learning centers are quite common now. Whole language teachers prefer centers organized around topics and thematic units, structured to facilitate the integration of all the language processes with conceptual learning. Specific writing centers or book centers are therefore equipped to facilitate ongoing units as well as general topics. In some skills-oriented programs, centers are places pupils go to do worksheets and skills exercises. That's why it's important for centers in whole language classrooms to be integrated and keyed to the ongoing whole language program.

Usually pupils organize their own distribution system. The whole language classroom is theirs, and if given an opportunity, they will ensure that materials are easily available and respected. They will set rules for getting and using materials and equipment, for moving around the room (and out of it). As always, the teacher is omnipresent, watching, mixing in, making sure that the whole language curriculum is not inhibited or blocked, and helping to settle disputes and uncertainties. But a pupil does not need special permission to check for spelling in a dictionary or another book. A small group decides for itself who should get a library book. A pupil asks a classmate to try out a phrase for the story she is writing, and does it without disturbing others.

Whole language materials

Basal readers, sequenced skill programs, or the usual types of instructional materials are really not needed. In fact, workbooks and duplicated skill exercises are inappropriate in whole language programs. What is appropriate is anything the children need or want to read or write. Lots of recreational books are needed, fiction and non-fiction, with a wide range of difficulty and interest, and resource materials of all kinds, some particularly prepared for use in school (like beginners' dictionaries and encyclopedias) and some "real world" resources (like phone books, TV guides, and adult reference books).

The money spent on reading, writing, spelling, and handwriting *texts can* be used to keep the classroom supplied with a rich range of authentic resources. Every classroom at every level needs a classroom library, augmented by book clubs and book exchanges, by groups of books borrowed from the public library, by short-term collections from the school library, and by student-authored books produced in the class publishing center. It's very important to have a wide range of books and other materials within immediate reach.

WHOLE LANGUAGE:
WHAT MAKES IT WHOLE?

Before we get to specifics, let's consider what distinguishes whole language approaches from other reading-writing methods. Most of the discussion will center on reading, simply because there has been so little teaching of writing, particularly in elementary schools. Perhaps no one could figure out how to make a basal writing series! So we have limited ourselves to isolated spelling and handwriting instruction. It should be said, however, that considerable writing in a holistic way is beginning to be done in elementary schools, mainly because of Donald Graves and his colleagues.

What is not whole language?

Teaching practices, reading programs, and curricula in schools vary widely at the moment, and many of them are simply incompatible with whole language instruction. Whole language firmly rejects such things as these:

- isolating skill sequences
- slicing up reading and writing into grade slices, each slice neatly following and dependent on prior ones

- simplifying texts by controlling their sentence structures and vocabulary, or organizing them around phonic patterns
- equating reading and writing with scores on tests of "sub-skills"
- isolating reading and writing instruction from its use in learning, or in actual reading and writing
- believing there are substantial numbers of learners who have difficulty learning to read or write for any physical or intellectual reason

Skills-technology views

Contemporary reading instruction has been dominated by several key factors:

The development of a technology of reading instruction
This technology grew between 1920 and 1960. Linguists, psycholinguists, and sociolinguists were busy elsewhere, and North American educators and researchers put great faith in technology. Behavioral psychology strongly dominated. The technology incorporated narrow views of language and language learning.

Tests: the focus of the technology
Standardized reading tests assume that reading can be subdivided neatly into sub-skills that can easily be sequenced and measured. Learning to read means scoring better on tests of these sequenced bits and pieces: letter-sound relationships, isolated words, abstract definitions, fractured sentences, and paragraphs pulled out of the middle of longer coherent texts. With faith in technology, teachers, school boards, and legislators came to rely more and more on tests. At their worst, tests decide promotion or failure, admission to special programs and ability tracks, and the effectiveness of teachers. In extreme cases, they have even become the curriculum. This very abusive use of tests has driven teachers to seek alternatives that are more positive, more humane and fairer to learners, more soundly based on modern research and theory, and more effective in producing learning. Teachers know they know more about their pupils than the tests can show them.

Basal readers in every classroom up to grade 8

Basals, basals, everywhere! Basals vary somewhat in the criteria used to organize and sequence them, but essentially they are organized around controlled vocabulary. So, learning to read becomes learning to recognize words: the most common words appear in primers and early books, while less common words are introduced gradually over the years; behavioral psychology is used to develop rules for how often a word must be repeated in a text once it is introduced, and how many words should be introduced per page; separate basals are created for each grade.

A view of words as the key units in learning to read and write

There have been noisy public battles between those advocating explicit phonics approaches and those advocating teaching words as wholes. The latter use a range of ways to "attack" words in order to learn them, including phonics. The former argue that once kids know "the sounds of the letters" they can read and don't need anything else. But both agree that learning to read is a matter of learning words. In fairness, it should be said that whole-word advocates tend to be more concerned with giving kids good stories. There are even some who have tried to combine a strong explicit phonics program with having the pupils read real stories.

Direct instruction for reading

The technology has produced workbooks, ditto masters, extra practice for learners who get low test scores, and supplementary "enrichment" materials for the high scorers. Strangely, the huge allocation of time for reading instruction does not mean that a lot of time is spent on actual reading. Little time is left after skills drill exercises, phonics drills, and workbook exercises with nothing longer than a line or two. Writing gets even less time, as does oral language, science, social studies, humanities, arts, or thinking about real problems.

Severely labeled children

Readers are labeled remedial, disabled, or dyslexic if they don't do well in tests and technologized reading programs. They then get more isolated drills on phonics and word attacks, and even less time for learning language while using language to learn. What they suffer from most is the fact of being labeled.

Dislike of reading

Large numbers have managed to survive the technology and learn to read and write with at least moderate effectiveness, but in the process have learned to think of reading and writing as unpleasant activities to be done only when absolutely necessary. They can read and write, but they usually choose not to do so if the choice is their own to make.

Breaking some icons

There are some aspects of the reading technology that have become so firmly entrenched in conventional reading instruction that they need special attention to indicate why they have no place in whole language programs:

Readiness

Some good reasons lay behind special readiness programs. Children need time to mature; rushing them is counter-productive. So when Washburne said that a mental age of 6 was necessary for success in learning to read, many people eagerly accepted that, though even at the time questions were raised about the validity of the research. Similarly, people could see that when children start school they haven't yet developed fine muscle control, so they should perhaps not be expected to write with adult pencils and pens. Unfortunately, bad reasoning combined these facts with a lack of understanding of human language development and use. What resulted were non-language activities and abstractions that had nothing to do with children's readiness for written language development.

Real readiness is intrinsic when language is real. Good kid-watchers know when children see a need for reading and writing, have confidence in themselves, and want to join "the literacy club." Whole language teachers don't rush children, but neither do they distract them from natural functional language use and development. They simply support them as they build on what they already know.

Phonics

Phonics is the set of relationships between the sound system of oral language and the letter system of written language. Phonics methods of teaching reading and writing reduce both to matching letters with sounds. It is a flat-earth view of the world, since it rejects modern science about reading and writing and how they develop. Phonics programs tend to be unscientific even in their presentation of phonic relationships. It simply isn't true that "when two vowels go walking, the first does the talking" except in a limited number of cases, which must be already known to the reader in order for the rule to be sensible.

Besides, English vowels don't just come in long and short varieties. The difference in the vowels in the following list of words will vary from dialect to dialect: *frog, fog, bog, dog, smog, cog, hog, jog.* But not one of the sounds is a "long o." Phonics programs can't deal with dialect differences unless they acknowledge that each dialect has a different set of phonics rules. Moreover, phonics methods ignore normal shifts in pronunciation that happen as words add affixes. Notice the letter "t" in *site, situate, situation.* The "t" stays in each word even though the sound shifts as the affixes are added. That's good, because it preserves the meaning relationship between these related words.

But even a more scientific phonics approach would be insufficient as a method for teaching reading and writing. The logic of phonics instruction is that letters can be coded as sounds, or sounds as letters. Then these can be blended to produce reading or writing. But that doesn't produce meaningful language — it only produces strings of sounds or letters.

Instead, children discover the alphabetic principle when they learn to write. There are relationships between letter patterns and sound patterns. They do what they do in all language learning: they search for rules. That leads to invented spelling. But spelling is standardized in English (and most other languages), so the rules produce only a possible spelling, not necessarily the standard one. Thus children learn to keep their eyes open for standard spellings as they read, and to suspend the rules when they don't work. Gradually they move toward conventional spelling in their writing.

Readers are seeking meaning, not sounds or words. They may use their developing phonics generalizations to help when the going gets tough. If they are lucky enough not to have been taught phonics in isolation, with each letter equally important, then they will not be diverted from developing the strategies necessary to select just enough graphic information to get to the sense they are seeking.

In a whole language program readers and writers develop control over the phonic generalizations in the context of using written language sensibly. These self-developed rules are not overlearned and artificial as they would be if they were imposed by a structured reading and spelling program. Whole language programs and whole language teachers do not ignore phonics. Rather they keep it in the perspective of real reading and real writing.

What are the principles of whole language?

Whole language is an attempt to get back to basics in the real sense of that word — to set aside basals, workbooks, and tests, and to return to inviting kids to learn to read and write by reading and writing real stuff.

Principles for reading and writing

- Readers construct meaning during reading. They use their prior learning and experience to make sense of the texts.
- Readers predict, select, confirm, and self-correct as they seek to make sense of print. In other words, they guess or make hypotheses about what will occur in the text. Then they monitor their own reading to see whether they guessed right or need to correct themselves to keep making sense. Effective reading makes sense. Efficient reading does it with the least amount of effort and input. Rapid readers tend to have high comprehension because they are both effective and efficient.
- Writers include enough information and detail so what they write will be comprehensible to their readers. Effective writing makes sense for the intended audience. Efficient writing includes only enough for it to be comprehensible.

- Three language systems interact in written language: the grapho-phonic (sound and letter patterns), the syntactic (sentence patterns), and the semantics (meanings). We can study how each one works in reading and writing, but they can't be isolated for instruction without creating non-language abstractions. All three systems operate in a pragmatic context, the practical situation in which the reading and writing is taking place. That context also contributes to the success or failure of the reading or writing.
- Comprehension of meaning is always the goal of readers.
- Expression of meaning is always what writers are trying to achieve.
- Writers and readers are strongly limited by what they already know, writers in composing, readers in comprehending.

Principles for teaching and learning

- School literacy programs must build on existing learning and utilize intrinsic motivations. Literacy is an extension of natural whole language learning: it is functional, real, and relevant.
- Literacy develops from whole to part, from vague to precise, from gross to fine, from highly concrete and contextualized to more abstract, from familiar contexts to unfamiliar.
- Expression (writing) and comprehension (reading) strategies are built during functional, meaningful, relevant language use.
- Development of the ability to control the form of reading and writing follows, and is motivated by, the development of the functions for reading and writing.
- There is no hierarchy of sub-skills, and no necessary universal sequence.
- Literacy develops in response to personal/social needs. Children growing up in literate environments become literate before they come to school.
- There is no one-to-one correspondence between teaching and learning. The teacher motivates, arranges the environment, monitors development, provides relevant and appropriate materials, and invites learners to participate in and plan literacy events and learning opportunities. Ultimately, it is the learner who builds knowledge, knowledge structures, and

strategies from the enriched environment the teacher helps to create.

- As teachers monitor and support the development of reading and writing strategies, learners focus on the communication of meaning. So there is a double agenda in literacy instruction. The kids focus on what they are using reading and writing for. The teachers focus on development and use.

- Risk-taking is essential. Developing readers must be encouraged to predict and guess as they try to make sense of print. Developing writers must be encouraged to think about what they want to say, to explore genre, to invent spellings, and to experiment with punctuation. Learners need to appreciate that miscues, spelling inventions, and other imperfections are part of learning.

- Motivation is always intrinsic. Kids learn to read and write because they need and want to communicate. Extrinsic rewards have no place in a whole language program. Punishment for not learning is even more inappropriate.

- The most important question a teacher can ask a reader or writer is, "Does that make sense?" Learners need to be encouraged to ask the same question of themselves as they read and write.

- Materials for instruction must be whole texts that are meaningful and relevant. From the first school experiences, they must have all the characteristics of real functional language. There is no need for special texts to teach reading or writing.

- Away with exercises that chop language into bits and pieces to be practiced in isolation from a whole text!

- Predictability is the real measure of how hard a text is for a particular reader. The more predictable, the easier.

- No materials are acceptable if they divert the attention of writers from expression and readers from comprehension.

What's whole about whole language?

We can summarize what's whole in whole language in the following points:
- Whole language learning builds around whole learners learning whole language in whole situations.

- Whole language learning assumes respect for language, for the learner, and for the teacher.
- The focus is on meaning and not on language itself, in authentic speech and literacy events.
- Learners are encouraged to take risks and invited to use language, in all its varieties, for their own purposes.
- In a whole language classroom, all the varied functions of oral and written language are appropriate and encouraged.

Evaluation

In all that, whole language teachers are concerned with helping learners build underlying competence. They have no interest in getting them to behave in predetermined ways in class and on tests. For example, spelling competence is not a matter of memorizing words for the Friday spelling test, but a matter of first trying out words as they are needed in writing, and then learning the limits of invented spelling against social convention. The basic competence of children who can comprehend when they read English is not reflected in tests of word recognition or phonics "skills." Moreover, pupils can give right answers on tests for wrong reasons, and wrong answers for right reasons. Whole language teachers know that the language miscues pupils make often show their underlying competence, the strengths they are developing and testing the limits of.

Kid-watching

Before the testing movement became the multi-million dollar activity it has become, there was a developing child-study movement among researchers and educators. It's simply true that one can learn much more about pupils by carefully watching than by formal testing. Whole language teachers are constant kid-watchers. Informally, in the course of watching a child write, listening to a group of children discuss or plan together, or having a casual conversation, teachers evaluate. It even happens while children are playing. It happens more formally in one-to-one conferences with pupils about their reading or writing, as teachers make anecdotal records of what they observe. It may involve instruments like the Reading Miscue Inventory or a writing observation form. The key is that it happens in the course of ongoing classroom activities.

Whole language teachers evaluate and revise their plans on the basis of the kid-watching they do. But the most useful form of evaluation is self-evaluation. Teachers continuously evaluate themselves and their teaching. They also help pupils develop ways of evaluating their own development, of knowing when they are and when they are not successful in using language and learning through it.

Evaluation has certain general purposes in any program. It is useful in planning and modifying instruction so it will be more effective. It is also useful in getting a sense of the progress pupils have made in their growth, and some sense of the needs they have. Most of these purposes can be accomplished through ongoing kid-watching.

At times it may be useful to use more formal devices to get indications of the strengths and weaknesses of the learners. Unfortunately, most standardized tests of reading and writing focus strongly on isolated skills and words. If they use connected texts, these are often short, disjointed, and deliberately obscure to make them harder, so that the scores are stretched out and produce a bell-shaped performance curve. To the extent that standardized tests test things other than effective use of language, they are inappropriate for judging whole language programs and useless in serving the legitimate aims of evaluation.

Instead, most whole language teachers have pupils fill portfolios with their own writing, records of their reading experiences, and examples of other learning activities.

DEVELOPING LITERACY:
WHOLE LANGUAGE THE WHOLE WAY

Whole language integrates oral and written language, and it integrates development in both with learning across the curriculum. In this chapter, notes on a more specific reading and writing program will be presented. Readers should keep in mind that everything said here about developing literacy assumes that it is being done in the context of an integrated holistic curriculum.

How can whole language be implemented?

Holistic instruction shows continuous respect for language, for learners, and for teachers. It begins with everyday, useful, relevant, functional language, and moves through a full range of written language including literature in all its variety.

One major advantage whole language approaches have over others is that they don't require special instructional materials. What's required is a range of real materials in the language(s) of the learners. The key to immersion programs in second-language learning is the fact that learners are involved in real speech and literacy events. It's as simple as that, and just as important in developing literacy as it is in developing oracy (control over oral language).

Children read familiar, meaningful wholes first, predictable materials that draw on concepts and experiences they already have: signs, cereal boxes, T-shirts, and books. Soon they will spot familiar words and phrases in new wholes, and it won't be long before they are able to handle unfamiliar words and phrases in familiar uses anywhere — with no worries for the teacher about a sequence or hierarchy of skills. The curriculum is organized through shared planning between teachers and pupils around real problem-solving, real ideas, and real relevant issues. Such an authentic curriculum presents many opportunities for making sense out of print or for writing comprehensibly. You can't make sense of or through language if the language isn't all available to you. Literacy development is a matter of getting the processes together: learning, in the context of reading and writing real language, to use just enough print, language structure, and meaning, and to keep it all in the proper personal and cultural perspective. Learners need to know which available cues are most useful in a particular written context. Trial and error, risk-taking on the part of the learner, is an absolute requirement. Pupils must become more flexible as they become involved with content further removed from their direct, personal experience.

There are no whole language literacy programs without whole language teachers. Most crucial is the new role of the enlightened teacher who serves as guide, facilitator, and kid-watcher. Whole language teachers try to help developing readers and writers use written language to learn — to acquire, extend, and present concepts. They capitalize on the language competence and the language learning ability of children, and help make literacy an extension of natural language learning. They know their pupils well, and encourage them to collaborate with their peers. These teachers share their own expertise and knowledge with their pupils.

Preschool literacy
Literacy begins with doing what other family members do already responding to signs, logos, and labels; sharing books; scribbling notes. Many children take books to bed and cuddle them like teddy bears. There's a ready market for board books, bathable books, and books to touch, smell, and manipulate. Children who have crayons, pencils, pens, or markers experiment avidly with writing.

Objectives

- Continue to build an awareness of the functions of print — environmental print, informational reading, note writing, recreational books.
- Create literate environments with functional print everywhere and children constantly encouraged to notice it, use it, and transact with it.
- Expand children's sense of books and how to handle them. Not all children will have had access to books, magazines, and other print materials. Now is the time to give them that.
- Expand children's sense of narrative and expository texts.
- Expand their sense of the style and form of written language. Children should be read to and with. Their composition should be encouraged through dictation to teachers and para-professionals, and through beginning attempts at personal writing.

Parents can play a vital role at this stage. Ask them to share with their children such things as letters, forms, advertisements, magazines, signs, packages, and other literacy events. Urge them to take their children to libraries, where, as soon as they can sign their own names, they can check out their own books.

Specifics

- Provide a writing corner with lots of different things to write with and on.
- Use written language to tell children what things mean and what they are for, and encourage them to guess what written language says.
- Use written communications between school and home, and make children aware of the messages they contain. Emphasize their importance as message carriers.
- Take walks around the neighborhood and look for environmental print. Ask: "Why is the print there?" "What does it say?"
- Use children's names in the classroom to create attendance charts and to label belongings. Have children sign in and put their belongings in

their personally labeled boxes or cubbies.

- Make charts and bulletin boards.
- Read to and with children individually and in small groups. Encourage them to follow, predict, read along, and even take over if they choose.
- Get lots of books: response books, activity books, wordless books.
- Create centers for listening to records or tapes and for writing grocery lists, notes, and picture captions.
- Encourage kids to play at reading and writing.
- Highlight the value of literacy during role-playing as children read recipes and cook, go to the corner store with a shopping list, or dress up at the clothes center where they write sales tickets or follow patterns.

Beginning literacy

The term "beginning literacy" here refers only to the beginning of a concerted school program to support growth into literacy. It fosters children's pride and confidence in their language(s) and their growing literacy. The program builds from whole to part, encouraging school beginners to be self-confident risk-takers.

Objectives

- Support developing awareness of print and its functions.
- Support the transition into productive reading.
- Build strategies, not specifics: meaning-seeking, predicting, inferencing, sampling, confirming, self-correcting in reading; inventing spellings and experimenting with forms to serve their functions in writing.
- Cultivate the alphabetic principle, not specific phonics.
- Develop risk-taking. In a whole language beginning literacy program, the teacher is monitor, cheerleader, co-reader, and facilitator.

Specifics

- Make the classroom itself a literate environment in which functional, meaningful, relevant language is everywhere.
- With pupils, label centers and write charts for rules, attendance, and jobs.
- Create a gallery of biographies of the children, written and read by them.
- Make charts and bulletin boards open-ended. When appropriate, have children add to them with letters from grandparents, favorite logos, book jackets they've made, precious collections, etc.
- Create stores with boxes, cartons, and signs, as well as a classroom post office where each child has a box for receiving mail and messages.
- Get the kids involved in reading whole meaningful texts right from the beginning. Wordless picture books such as *The Red Balloon* or *Pancakes for Breakfast* help to build a sense of books and of narrative.
- Encourage children to dictate stories or experiences, individually or in groups, to an adult who writes for them. Then have the children read back their own texts. These may be rewritten on charts for further use, or bound at a classroom publishing center.
- Choose one or more read-along activities:

    A common home read-along has the child sitting on an adult's lap looking at the book the adult is reading aloud. The adult stops or fades out periodically and lets the child take over. There are now commercial versions of this lap method that promote shared book experiences in school.

    Many whole language teachers set up listening centers where children can listen through earphones to tapes or records while following the text in a book.

    Others use "big book" versions of popular books that allow several children to see the same text and join in a choral reading with a leader — the teacher, another adult, or a classmate. Several companies now offer big book kits that include normal-sized copies along with the big book.

Assisted reading is a more formal read-along approach in which the teacher first reads with the child and then gradually shifts to merely supporting and assisting as the child reads the familiar story/text.

Sing-along charts and choral reading of poems also enrich co-reading in the classroom.

Reading and writing

The best books at this stage are predictable books. Their familiar content and structure, and the often repetitious, cyclical sequencing make them predictable. *This is the House That Jack Built* or *I Know an Old Lady Who Swallowed a Fly* are good examples. It's easy for kids to get a sense of where the book is going and to predict what is coming next. Fortunately, young children seem to love rereading familiar predictable materials, which gives them lots of productive, self-motivated practice.

From the beginning, children write for themselves as well as dictate to teachers. They write predictable books of their own in frank imitation of the patterns of some of their favorites. They tape their own sing-alongs and choral readings to add to their taped-book collections. Reading and writing develop together and support each other. Young writers learn to read like writers: they notice surprising spellings, become alert to style and structure, and know that books have authors because they've experienced authoring themselves.

They also integrate reading and writing experiences into their thematic units and their search for knowledge across the curriculum. So they learn to read and write expository language as well. They learn to enjoy and create a good story, but they also learn to describe, to report, to raise questions and answer them, to share real experiences. They write letters, keep journals, make signs, labels, and lists. They keep records of their own physical growth, and the growth and food intake of classroom pets. They read the school lunch menu, the TV guide, the weather report, and keep the class up to date on the latest information.

Beginners are encouraged to take risks. When they write they spell words as best they can, inventing if necessary, but using the words they need when they need them rather than sticking with those they are sure they can spell. Their reading miscues are celebrated if they contribute to making sense and show developing strategies. No one is perfect, and sense rather than error-free performance is the main point of reading. The teacher helps them see that they should not tolerate nonsense when they read.

The teacher also monitors development through close observation. The children are growing into readers and writers. From the beginning, the reading and writing is theirs through authentic literacy events for real purposes. They have and maintain a sense of ownership — they are not tenants in someone else's literacy program. They aren't acquiring skills for later use. Rather, they are reading and writing because they need and want to do so.

Handwriting

The act of producing writing is laborious for young children and requires a great deal of physical coordination. That's the reason for using manuscript writing. Cursive writing takes more coordination and is more prone to illegibility, particularly for beginners. Even for adults, cursive handwriting becomes so idiosyncratic, so personalized, that it may become illegible. Typewriters and word processors have largely replaced handwritten letters and written texts in business.

In the beginning, composition can simply involve young pupils dictating to an adult who transcribes for later reading. Also, word processors with easy-to-learn software have been successfully used with school beginners in recent years: they take much of the drudgery out of the writing and children produce much longer texts. A few English schools are now using a simple five button keyboard, the Quinkey.

Whole language teachers understand that handwriting is not a skill that can be learned first and then used. Instruction in letter formation is built into real literacy events. Control will take a while, and development will be characterized by miscues and imperfections. Although there are many variations in physical coordination, teachers encourage all kids to write and keep on writing even if it's hard to do so legibly. Nothing discourages struggling young writers so much as a bulletin board full of near perfect but copied exercises with a label something like "Our Best Work."

Left-handed pupils need special support and encouragement. Left-handed writing doesn't need to look right-handed. It has characteristics of its own, since the writing hand will be in a different position relative to the body and the paper. Furthermore, left-handed writers are at a disadvantage learning from and watching right-handed teachers, particularly if the teachers are insensitive.

Fortunately, experienced kid-watchers easily spot how writing does or doesn't contribute to effective expression. They keep coordination, handedness, legibility, and conformity to conventions in perspective.

Developmental literacy

Developmental literacy encompasses the major part of school programs: the expansion of efficiency and effectiveness in readers and writers, and of flexibility in using literacy for various purposes. Again, developing readers and writers must be involved in authentic literacy events and in a wide range of real comprehensible texts, and they must be in control of their own use and development of literacy.

Objectives

- Build pupils' level of confidence and encourage risk-taking. Pupils self-select materials to read, strive to comprehend what they read, and risk using writing to communicate.
- Expand pupils' flexibility and help them broaden and refine their taste and breadth of interests.
- Support the development of effective expression and comprehension strategies.
- Help pupils build efficient reading and writing in a wide range of functional contexts.
- Support pupils' growth in their ability to learn through written language.
- Build a love of reading and writing so that pupils will choose to do both during their leisure time, as sources of pleasure and aesthetic satisfaction.

Specifics

These are the keys: lots of reading and writing, risk-taking to try new functions for reading and writing, focusing on meaning. If these three essentials aren't present, no matter how many specific whole language activities are used, the program will not be a successful whole language program.

Self-selection

Pupils are helped to broaden the scope and range of their reading and writing and to build the special strategies needed for different kinds of texts used for different purposes. It helps if students know what they want to know, what questions they want answered, and what problems they need to solve.

Sustained time for reading and writing

Many diligent teachers find it hard to stay out of the kids' way. We think we're not teaching if we're not telling them something, or at least asking them something. But watching them as they read and write is often more helpful. Of course teachers need to know what the kids are doing and be there when they need (and particularly when they ask for) help. But much can be accomplished through regular individual conferences where the pupils share their reading and writing with the teacher, through small group interactions, and through peer editing conferences.

Journals

Teachers respond regularly to what kids write. As they get older, pupils may prefer to turn their journals into private diaries, and they should decide whether or not the teacher will read and respond.

A variation from Japan uses writing to have children get in touch with themselves. There teachers believe that beginning writing should narrate the child's own experiences, to help put the child in touch with his or her feelings. They do not respond except to comment on the extent to which the young writers are coming to grips with the experiences they've had and their reactions to them.

Process writing

Donald Graves, Donald Murray, Lucy Caulkins, and others have developed this approach. Young writers are allowed time for pre-writing, for thinking about and planning what they will say. Then there is time for the writing. Finally, there is time to share with classmates what was written. Getting responses from a real peer audience is helpful in revision.

Revision

Many things kids write — notes to friends, quick responses to experiences, jottings, or journal entries — serve their purposes in their initial forms. Revisions are reserved for stories, reports, personal narratives, or expressions of personal response to ideas or experiences, whatever is intended for sharing with a wider audience. Revision helps make the text more comprehensible and acceptable to the intended audience. It also helps writers say what they intend to say. The process of revision also leads to more effective strategies for expression and to more successful texts. It's important to develop a sense of what kinds of text need revision under what circumstances, and what the best devices are for revising each text type.

Spelling, punctuation, and forms

There is simply no doubt that, as long as they keep on writing meaningfully, young writers will move toward conventional spelling and punctuation, and control over the forms of stories, letters, and other writing genres.

Spelling: Beginners will generate spellings so minimal and unique that even they may not always be able to read what they've written. But soon they will develop predictable consistencies so that both they and the teacher can read what they write. In English, for example, vowels will initially be left out, and then some vowels will consistently represent vowel sounds that are not necessarily the conventional ones. Soon even readers who are not as experienced as teachers with invented spellings will be able to figure out what the writer is saying.

Next, developing writers will realize that the spelling in the material they read is standardized. This may inhibit their writing, as they avoid using words they're not sure of. But if they feel supported and encouraged, they will continue to invent spellings for new words they need, while using their reading and writing experience to move toward conventional spelling. Studies of misspellings among young writers show that they are almost entirely confined to words being used for the first time. Frequently used words are only infrequently misspelled.

Punctuation: The same story. If they read and if they write, kids develop a sense for where to punctuate. There's no way to rush it, but there's no need to hurry anyway. Just don't tell kids that periods come at the end of sentences and then teach them that sentences end with periods!

Forms of writing: Pupils learn about basic forms of writing by using them. For example, they learn to write a letter, for either formal or informal purposes, by writing real letters to real people for real reasons. Whole language classrooms have mailboxes, and children write to each other. They are also encouraged to write to relatives, to friends, or to companies for information. Arranging for written exchanges with other classrooms or groups provides real literacy events involving handwriting.

Meaning in reading

In reading, meaning is always both input and output. First, wanting to comprehend is half the battle. Of course the conceptual load must be appropriate and the writing must be quality stuff, but pupils will work hard and extend themselves to understand texts that are important to them. Pupils are active in their own learning and transactive with the texts they read.

It's important to recognize the limits of textbooks. Good ones support the curriculum, but holistic teachers do not abuse and misuse textbooks by equating them with the curriculum. They use them as limited resources and build cooperative relationships with librarians, publishers, and authors, so that students can become aware of the large variety of written language resources they can use to build the knowledge they are looking for.

Skills and strategies

The technology of reading boasts of objective skills and drills. Instead, whole language programs offer development of comprehension strategies. These focus on the ways living, breathing people organize graphic, syntactic, and meaning cues for making sense of real whole language. The human mind constantly develops strategies for organizing the information it needs for all kinds of purposes. Whole language programs use strategy lessons to expand on strengths and help build strategies.

Strategy lessons require the use of meaningful language passages in the context of real literacy events. Many different types are rapidly being developed. Here is an example:

A teacher notes that some pupils tend to substitute *what* for *that* when they read. There are also occasional *when/then* and *where/there* substitutions, often in situations where either word would fit. Rather than drilling on isolated words, the teacher finds — or writes — a meaningful passage in which each time only one of the words can fit and make sense. The pupils read the passage to strengthen their self-correction strategies. With each miscue, they discover something is wrong and are led by the text to correct. But this strategy lesson also helps them become better predictors. It's important not to call their attention to the words in isolation, since that would compound the problem by strengthening an association between the words.

Metacognition

Recently, some researchers have discussed metacognition: knowing what you know and how you know it. They argue that comprehension and expression will be aided by getting kids to talk about the literacy processes. The idea that kids are helped by being taught *first* about language is not consistent with the basic whole language principle. However, it probably is true that as kids become literate they get some key insights about reading and writing which subsequently make their learning easier. Among these are:

- Language is always supposed to make sense. So in reading you know you've been successful if you understand what you read. In writing you keep rereading what you've written to make sure it makes sense.

- No one can understand everything. This reality can help kids maintain their self-confidence and develop some sense of when their lack of comprehension is the fault of the text, their lack of background, or other sources besides their own reading ability.
- Personal meanings may differ from the meanings of the community, in minor or major ways. Pupils need to internalize these shared meanings while maintaining and perfecting their personal meanings.

Teachable moments

They're the best for metacognition. Sometimes one or more pupils want to talk about language. Sometimes teachers can evoke curiosity about an aspect of language. In either case, the goal of the teacher is to help pupils use their insights to build comprehension and expression strategies.

Strategies across the curriculum

Learners need to develop special strategies for comprehending the kinds of text found in math, science, social studies, and the arts. For instance, it helps when they discover that math story problems need to be read in several ways for several purposes:

- deciding what information is being sought
- laying out a solution strategy and deciding on appropriate equations and computations
- getting specific information and checking the potential solution against the problem

Literacy development in a content area

Here is a general approach:

- Review the general and special uses of reading and writing in the content area.
- Consider what kinds of written language texts are common in the field, particularly those pupils may not have encountered before: for example, maps, charts, recipes, directions, job sheets, scripts.

- Think through and list what strategies, background knowledge, and special resources are needed to reproduce and comprehend the texts the field uses.
- Determine where kids are in being able to meet these needs.
- Plan the double agenda that will build the necessary language strategies while building knowledge in the subject area.

REVALUING:
AN ALTERNATIVE TO REMEDIATION

When pupils don't do well in a technologized reading and writing program, it's assumed there must be something wrong with *them*. The language of medical pathology will describe it: reading disabilities, dyslexia, diagnosis, clinics, prescriptions, treatments, remediation. We blame their eyes, their brains, their central nervous systems, their diets, their noisy homes or their quiet ones, their neglectful parents or their over-anxious ones. But after all the diagnosis, the treatment is remarkably uniform: take two phonics exercises three times a day. That's because the pathology of reading failure knows nothing about the reading process or reading development.

Writing deficiencies don't often cause alarm before high school. The early assumption is that if kids can't read there's no point in expecting them to write. In high schools we "know" that students write poorly because they haven't been taught to write correctly. Resulting exercises in writing form, spelling, and handwriting produce even more uptight writers who try to write by the rules instead of trying to say something in writing. College remedial writing courses continue to be atomistic and negative and to focus on form rather than meaningful language.

A whole language perspective is bluntly opposed to all that. Language learning is not difficult. If young humans haven't succeeded in becoming literate in school, something must be wrong with the program: *it* needs remediation, not they.

In the meantime, there are lots of ineffective and troubled readers and writers. You easily recognize them. They are often in conflict with themselves and are usually their own worst enemies. By now they try to read and write by busily attacking words and looking up spellings. They mistrust their own language strategies and become dependent on teachers to tell them what to do as they read and write. They are reluctant to take the necessary risks, with the result that their reading and writing looks far less competent than it actually is. They believe that everyone knows they are literacy failures, and they act the part.

They believe there are two kinds of people in school: those who can read and write and those who can't and never will. They think the skills and drill exercises that never work for them always work for the good readers, who never have any problems. It's all their own fault — a sign of something defective, inferior, or bad. They suffer from the "next word" syndrome. Every word they're not sure of is proof that they are bad readers. Good readers always know the next word. All words are equal, aren't they? So they sound out every proper name, as well as the important concept-carrying words. They don't expect things to make sense. Reading is the tedious task of trying to get all the words right. They believe that good writers are perfect spellers too, so what's the use of even trying.

They also suffer from the "I can't remember" syndrome. Good readers have total recall of everything they read, of course. Since these readers never do, they're defective. Troubled writers have never heard of "composition at the point of utterance." They believe good writers have the whole of what they will write in their heads before they begin.

It's easy to see how the technology of reading instruction, the tests, texts, and exercises, build these self-destructive and inaccurate views of literacy.

Children who have trouble in reading and writing do have strengths — making sense of language is natural for people. But through lack of self-confidence and overkill on isolated skills, they don't recognize their own strengths. They think their use of legitimate comprehension and expression strategies is cheating. They feel guilty if they make sense of what they're reading without sounding out the words, if they skip words and enjoy their reading without worrying about remembering everything.

Objectives

There are only two objectives of a revaluing program:

- To support pupils in revaluing themselves as language learners, and to get them to believe they are capable of becoming fully literate.
- To support pupils in revaluing reading and writing as functional, meaningful whole language processes rather than as sequences of sub-skills to be memorized.

Revaluing is essential. If those pupils are to become literate, they must lose the loser mentality. They must find the strength and confidence to take the necessary risks, to make the literacy choices, and to enter into functional literacy events. Whole language teaching helps pupils value what they can do and not be defeated by what they can't do; it helps them trust themselves and their linguistic intuitions, to become self-reliant in their sense of what they are reading.

Whole, relevant, meaningful language can help them move away from next-word fear, phonics, and word attacks. It can help them build productive meaning-seeking strategies. Eventually they will come to realize that making sense is all that reading and writing are about.

Specifics

Patience is a key word. Severely labeled pupils will take a while to turn around and start believing in themselves. The transition will require a building up of their understanding of what print can do for them in the context of real literacy events. In such contexts, they will gradually reveal to themselves and their teachers the strengths that have been hidden by the heavy layer of their own defeatism, brought on by inappropriate overuse of word-attack skills. But it will take time. Their scars are deep; the effect of years of pathological treatment and remediation will not wear off easily.

Beginner whole language activities are appropriate at any age, provided the content and interest level are relevant to the learners. Teenagers interested in cars can dictate to a teacher or tutor how to change a tire. When it has been typed or written, teacher and pupil can read it together. Perhaps this could initiate an auto mechanic's log or journal written by a group of pupils for their own use or that of others. Having troubled readers read along with a recorded reader, or read highly predictable materials are also useful techniques.

Materials of great interest are likely to be most predictable for learners, and the range of interests and experiences will become increasingly broad with age. Predictability will differ from person to person, since it depends on interests, culture, hobbies, vocations, values, and life experiences. Resourceful teachers get newspapers, magazines, books, forms, menus, or any other written texts to which they can point specific learners for specific purposes. Bless caring librarians! Bless patient teachers who never flag in believing that readers can predict and comprehend when they read about things they know! Their charges are prone to giving up easily and need constant reassurance.

Even with highly meaningful materials, it takes time for kids to revalue themselves and the processes of literacy. Teachers must expect some setbacks and even some trauma as learners struggle with themselves to accept that getting the gist of what they are reading is more important than getting each word right. Helping kids revalue themselves is largely helping them put themselves together. Over the years they've been fractionated, and have lost the sense of the whole. Keeping them involved, always, in a search for meaning eventually brings them together.

Pupils can also be encouraged to learn from their own miscues. They can work in pairs, taking turns reading and tape-recording their reading. At first the teacher listens to the tape, asks them about the miscues they notice they made, and encourages them to evaluate what they did right. Later they can work with their partners without the teacher's help. Self-appraisal helps to legitimize the miscue-making, guessing, predicting, and inferencing they are doing. The importance of self-correction in seeking to make sense of the text becomes clear. High-quality miscues are highlighted and suggestions are made that strategies which worked in some places could have been used in others to overcome similar difficulties. Working in pairs helps kids realize that others share their problems. Most of all, this self-analysis gets them to confront the reality of their own reading, including its strengths as well as its weaknesses, and that will make them question the stereotype of themselves as total losers in literacy.

These pupils often show progress in revaluing themselves as writers before they do as readers. They start keeping journals, and the entries get longer and longer. They are surprised and pleased to discover that people enjoy hearing about episodes in their lives, and they begin to write long accounts of interesting experiences. Writing is easy for new believers in themselves because it demands no skill prerequisites. Spelling, handwriting, and mechanics are learned on the job in the process of expressing. And their writing goes through the same remarkable rapid development that younger writers show, provided the teacher is there to be an interested consumer. The teacher must support and cheer them on and not wipe out their first efforts and early enthusiasm with red-penciled sarcasm. It's not lowering any standards to compliment a fourteen-year-old beginning writer on his first coherent six-page story, even if it does have some misspelled words and non-standard punctuation. If the writing continues, the rest will follow. If it doesn't, there won't be anything to spell or punctuate.

Preventive whole language

If kids are in whole language programs with whole language teachers right from the beginning, there are going to be a lot fewer readers and writers in trouble. Whole language teachers work at developing the full range of language functions in the context of the culture(s) of the learners. They are effective kid-watchers who see quickly when kids are not developing and find alternatives that will turn them on and get them moving. Most important, they believe in kids, and they believe kids have what it takes to become literate. They won't blame them for their lack of success. Rather, they'll build on their strengths and encourage them to believe in themselves and their ability to become literate.

REALITY:
THE STATE OF THE LANGUAGE ARTS

We're a long way from where we should be. Whole language teachers, schools, and policies in the English-speaking nations are increasing in numbers, but the three are not always found together. Sometimes school policy-makers have committed themselves, but the teachers were never involved and are now unable or unwilling to implement the programs. More common, whole language teachers alone and in small numbers try building whole language programs amidst unsupportive or even hostile administrator and curricular policies. Many parents support whole language administrative policies and teacher initiatives, but there is not yet a popular movement. Ultimately, if whole language is going to become the dominant school program, most parents must come to see the advantage of its humanistic/scientific base and its positive view of children and learning, and the potential it has for expanding both the effectiveness of their children's use of oral and written language and their ability to learn through language.

Well-developed ideas like whole language ought to be causing excitement, discussion, and controversy. They should be reflected in policies curriculum guides, published classroom materials, teacher education programs, and the professional and popular press. They are in many parts of the English-speaking world. For instance, language across the curriculum is a central concept in secondary programs in New Zealand, Britain, Canada, Australia, and such countries as Singapore, where English is one of the official languages. The United States, however, is lagging far behind.

What is happening in whole language?

New Zealand

For its single national school authority, whole language *is* the policy in New Zealand. Its secondary language program aims to:

- increase students' ability to understand and use language effectively.
- extend their imaginative and emotional responsiveness to and through language.
- extend their awareness of ideas and values through language.

Teachers are expected to develop programs consistent with these broad aims. They are asked to plan with their students "an appropriate range of language situations arising from and widening the students' own experience" — that is, expanding the range of language situations in which they are confident and competent. Teachers are expected to plan language activities based on students' everyday lives, widening interests, and developmental needs.

Evaluation is based on a full range of language use in different situations, rather than on tests: logs, folders, and tapes of work; records of teacher/student conferences; careful and continued observation of such activities as role-playing, group discussion, the making of collages and sound pictures; informal tests; assessment by audiences of class plays, debates, and other such language activities.

Great Britain

In 1975, the Bullock Committee, an official representation of the British government, issued its report called A *Language for Life*. It called for major changes in objectives, curricula, and methodology in education based on insights into the relationships among language, thinking, and learning. The report elevated concern for development of language and thinking to the level of policy. It was widely discussed in many English-speaking countries.

Since then, schools and local education authorities have established school language policies in Great Britain, Canada, Australia, and New Zealand. The school's acceptance of all forms of language and its commitment to support home languages as well as English have been clarified. The joint responsibility of the entire school staff for language development has been articulated. These policies make language a major focus of concern and put it at the center of the curriculum.

Also, many British teacher education programs have made language a major focus. James Britton, Nancy Martin, John Dixon, Harold Rosen, and Margaret Spencer are prominent British teacher educators who have played a major role in ensuring that British primary and secondary teachers have the background in language and learning they need to integrate language development with learning through language. There is now a broad process of holistic innovation there, though the *term* whole language is only beginning to be heard.

Canada

There has been a strong movement in Canada for whole language at many different levels. *English Language Arts I-VI* is the official policy statement of the Direction Générale de Development Pédagogique, Ministère de l'Education for the Province of Quebec. It mandates a "whole language, child-centered, integrated approach." Its core is a parallel series of theoretical assumptions and instructional principles. For example:

Theoretical assumption: language learning is an active developmental process which occurs over a period of time.

Instructional principle: children need time to internalize the process by actively engaging in the process of speaking, listening, reading, and writing.

Theoretical assumption: language arts must occur and flourish in literate environments where language users are free to discover and to realize their intentions.

Instructional principle: children need to be encouraged to take risks and need to experience varied opportunities for language use.

The teacher is asked to create meaningful contexts for learning, "invitational, emulative environments" which:

- provide integrated experiences with the language arts.
- influence the children's attitude toward language, while promoting development through developmentally appropriate varied opportunities for language use.
- support the natural process of learning, building language and extending knowledge, shaping meaning, and sharing the world of language.

The program ties broad objectives to related content. For the student to view English as a dynamic and living language, a wide range of stories, poems, plays, books, magazines, and newspapers should be at hand. Monitoring achievement includes two forms: response indicators like "reads every day," "recreates stories"; value indicators like "enjoys the different uses of language by authors." Evaluation suggestions include use of observation, formal and informal tests, parent and student conferences, school records, checklists, questionnaires, inventories, and tapes of oral language. Self-evaluation is integrally involved in the process and is encouraged.

A team of teachers in Edmonton, Alberta, has developed a working paper that has these premises:

Language Arts must be integrated, based on interdependence of listening, speaking, reading, and writing and the need for people to have language to communicate with others and understand and control their daily experiences. Language and thought develop together and subject area concepts develop at the same time as pupils' ability to express their understandings through reading and writing. Language is an active process learned through its use.

The statement of "Language Arts Outcomes" is both broad enough and specific enough to give direction to teachers and planners. It does not confuse trivial activities with reasons for learning. Here are some examples of their objectives:

- Students can and will read, listen, and view for recreation and information.
- Students are able to use language to discuss when constructing their own messages and analyzing the messages of others.

However, the Edmonton group recognizes that the program will not succeed unless teachers understand it, accept it enthusiastically, and are free to implement it.

Whole language views are represented in official documents and innovative practices all across Canada — in British Columbia, Alberta, Manitoba, Saskatchewan, Ontario, Quebec, Nova Scotia, New Brunswick, and Newfoundland. The David Livingston school in inner city Winnipeg has become a center of whole language teaching. Its staff and a group of associated Winnipeg educators have played a major role in creating a grassroots movement in Canada through in-service work.

The United States

There is a strong whole language movement in the United States, but it is harder to see against the background of irrational demands for excellence that only translate into standardized test scores, back-to-basics movements, and pressures for narrowed curricula from moral majority and elitist groups. John Goodlad calls a "monstrous hypocrisy" the "gap between rhetoric of individual flexibility, originality, and creativity in our educational goals and the cultivation of these goals in our schools ..." He says that "the emphasis on individual performance and achievement would be more conducive to cheating than to development of moral integrity," and concludes that "back to basics is where we've always been." In reading, he sees overwhelming focus on textbooks and workbooks, with little actual reading and writing. Excluding "the common practice of students taking turns reading from a common text," reading accounts for only 6% of elementary class time and trails off to 3% in junior high school and 2% in senior high.

Unlike the other countries we've looked at, whole language remains overwhelmingly a teachers' movement in the United States. Only a limited number of curriculum workers, administrators, and teacher educators actively support it.

How can policy become practice?

What must be done? The key problem is turning whole language policy into practical reality in the classroom. After all, whole language ideas and concepts become reality only at the point where a teacher is alone with a group of learners. Only there does a whole language program really exist.

But doing so won't be easy. Mechanistic, technological packages are popular among many school administrators. One American federally funded educational laboratory boasted that it took only a day to train (their word) teachers to use their program. Training consisted mostly of rehearsing the use of the script, which had an invariant format. Teachers were admonished not to deviate from the program in any way, for any child, for any reason. Another mastery learning program literally requires teachers to sign a loyalty oath to the program.

Whole language can't be packaged in a kit or bound between the covers of textbooks or workbooks. It certainly can't be scripted. There's no use building a whole language program without the support of the teachers. Teachers must reach their own informed professional decisions. They — with the kids — create whole language classrooms. Responsible administrators and curriculum planners have learned that teachers deserve the same humane, patient understanding as the pupils they teach. They can't be, and shouldn't be, coerced or intimidated.

"Support for Instructional Development" is the name of a new type of in-service program in the Albuquerque public schools. A major element is the support of study groups. Teachers are paid an hourly rate to participate in a series of seven or eight sessions. They are asked to read articles, keep journals to reflect on their reading, and ask questions. One series of lectures, discussions, and demonstrations focused on: beliefs about reading; word perception and using predictable materials; the schema theory and the socio-psycholinguistic nature of reading; making reading easy/literature as the content of reading; the reading/writing connection; miscue analysis; synthesis and reactions.

The support also extends to classroom demonstrations, in-service to entire school faculties, lunch symposia, individual staff/teacher conferences, location of materials and/or information, arranging visitations by teachers to other classrooms and other schools. This way more and more whole language teachers become willing and able to share what they know. Seeing what peers have done makes clear to novices that whole language works with kids exactly like the ones in their classes. Also, peer support lowers the risks for the teacher being supported because the peer has no intimidating authority.

American school systems might borrow ideas from England, where Moira McKenzie of the Inner London Education Authority runs courses. Some classroom teachers are released from classes to attend; some attend after a full day's teaching. The ILEA designates a few as "postholders in language." These are regular classroom teachers who have the responsibility of sharing ideas with their colleagues and supporting them in turn. The course creates a continuous, relatively non-threatening source of ideas, support and impetus for change.

In Great Britain, Australia, New Zealand, and Canada it is common to "second" teachers to a teacher center, a special project, or a teacher education program. The teacher performs a different professional role and at the same time acquires new insights and competences. Such borrowings happen in the United States too, but less frequently and less officially.

Curriculum guidelines

The Quebec curriculum guide and course of study provides an excellent model for a system-wide whole language program. Composing such a document takes as wide a range of participation as possible. Classroom teachers, specialists and support staff, curriculum workers and administrators, parents and other interested members of the community are all prime candidates for membership in committees and study groups. The support of teacher educators should also be enlisted. The process of developing a guideline is likely to be as important as the end product, and those who have had a hand in its development may make all the difference in its implementation later.

In presenting the completed guide to those who weren't involved, the developers should explain what decisions were made, why the guide is what it is, and what changes to the system the planners visualize. Teachers should explain to teachers, principals to principals, parents to parents.

Here are some of the things you might expect in a curriculum guide:

- A *language policy* that deals with the broad objectives of expanding oral and written language effectiveness in both English and mother-tongues. It should deal with general principles such as integrating language development with learning through language. But it should also tackle specific concerns of the population served, such as treatment of minority dialects. Bryant Fillion suggests that a language policy should deal with such things as: how students are required, encouraged, and permitted to use language; what happens as a result of their language use; and what they are taught — directly and indirectly — about language. Fillion argues for each school to explicate its language policy to demonstrate that it promotes "real language development and the effective use of language as a tool for learning."

- A *base of humanistic/scientific principles* to be used for choosing materials, planning instruction, organizing classrooms, and evaluating pupil progress and the program itself.

- *Methods* schools will use to expand and support learning. It should indicate the role of the teacher in supporting, facilitating, and monitoring language development, and suggest ways of integrating the language arts and establishing the double agenda of learning through language while learning language. Specific suggestions for organizing thematic units and for appropriate unit topics and resources will always be helpful. It should provide lists of fiction and non-fiction titles that can support unit topics. It should suggest appropriate language experiences (speech and literacy events) for units.

- *Recommendations* for time and space for a whole language program. Teachers are always worried that pupils will not have enough to do without workbooks and skills exercises. A guide should suggest a variety of ways to organize time in relationship to ongoing thematic units, so that pupils are productively involved and the teacher can monitor how they are using their time. It should also suggest how to develop centers, arrange desks, and make materials available and accessible so they will facilitate activity in an orderly manner.

- A *means of evaluation* is always a major concern, particularly in the United States with its almost obsessive preoccupation with the use of standardized tests, and any guide must address the problem. There is a model, developed by a group of teachers, which suggests a variety of informal and formal procedures and devices for monitoring the progress pupils are making in language and conceptual development (Marek, 1983).

The curriculum guide should be considered provisional and there should be a continuous process of revision and evaluation. This will permit the whole staff to feel that the curriculum is theirs and that their experience in facilitating whole language is important in shaping the program.

Whole language schools

Increasingly, whole schools are shifting to whole language programs, as a faculty decides that whole language is the way to go. Sometimes support is available from the local education authority or from a university faculty. In a few cases, parents and teachers have argued that if a basics program is a parental choice for some children, a positive holistic program should be a parental choice for others.

Liz Waterland describes how a program was established in Northborough School in Cambridgeshire, England:

No one in the school had used anything other than a conventional, largely skill-based program . . . There were the parents to worry about; their expectation would be that their children would follow the traditional pattern . . . There were the resources to consider. It was obvious that reading schemes were, with few exceptions, no longer appropriate. Had we sufficient books to use? What about children's writing? . . .

We already had a language curriculum. Now I wanted to abandon that plan; plainly the staff would also need to understand and support, at least in theory . . . It was the fact that my head teacher gave me his wholehearted support . . . that finally convinced me it could be done.

It was in this spirit that I began to attempt to turn theory into practice, first ... by myself feeling my way into it. Within a term, so successful was the children's response that colleagues in the rest of the school began using the apprenticeship approach with their classes. Two years later we were offering help to and sharing ideas with other schools throughout Cambridgeshire.

Waterland informed the parents right from the beginning, and asked them to support the program by reading with their children. Guidance was provided in a booklet: "... the home can offer time, individual attention, consistent support, and loving concern; the school can offer expertise, suitable texts, and understanding of progression."

The staff of David Livingstone school in Winnipeg, Manitoba, led by principal Orin Cochrane, plan and continuously revise the program. When they began, they had the support of Ethel Buchanan, who operates a teacher center. Team-teaching is common. The school is in an inner-city area with low income families, many of them native Canadians. With like-minded teachers, the staff forms a support group that provides courses and in-service workshops for teachers and administrators in other schools and other parts of the country.

The federally funded Chapter 1 Reading Program became the focus for initiating a whole language program in Albuquerque, New Mexico. Professor Bess Altwerger was selected to work a third of her time helping the staff of the Alamosa School. Administrator Virginia Resta facilitated and supported the plans. The school had recognized a great need for improvement in its literacy program. With support from the principal, a group of teachers volunteered to provide a whole language program. An on-site "facilitating teacher" was selected for coordination. Non-Chapter 1 teachers were encouraged to observe and participate, but there was no pressure.

In each example above, several key things were present:

- A staff that wanted to change to a positive, humanistic/scientific approach.
- A core of leadership within the group or supportive of it.
- The support of administrators who were not afraid to share power with teachers.
- Informed parents who supported the program.
- A knowledge-base which the staff was committed to, which was continually expanded, and which was actively used to build the program.
- Teachers who viewed themselves as professionals, who were not afraid to take risks, and who were willing to take responsibility for their classrooms.
- Pupils who participated in planning their education, who were actively engaged in their own development and the pursuit of knowledge, and who liked going to school.

Helping teachers change

Being a whole language teacher raises the level of professional authority and responsibility. It means accepting the responsibility of staying informed, of developing a sound base for classroom planning, practice, and decision-making. It is important, therefore, that support be continuous and long-term. Teachers must not feel abandoned after they've been convinced to change what they're doing, but before they know what to do instead.

It would be unfair, unrealistic, and unwise to expect teachers to make abrupt changes. They have reasons for what they do now. They know how successful (and unsuccessful) they are. They can predict from past experience how well something they do will work (and not work). Trying out new ways of doing things is risky business. The results are unpredictable. Teachers need support in setting their own pace and planning their own transition. If they need to cling to textbooks for a while, if they're not quite ready to let go of their formal spelling programs, that's all right. Conferences and support groups, support staff observations, and visits to other classrooms will help them think through what they are hanging onto, where they are inconsistent and where not, and how to keep moving ahead to more effective teaching.

WHOLE LANGUAGE:
NOT WITHOUT A
WHOLE LANGUAGE TEACHER

In the end there is no getting away from this truth: it's one class at a time, just you and your kids.

Most whole language teachers are not in whole language schools. They are often alone and frequently considered by their colleagues and administrators as hard-working and effective, but misguided. The lucky ones have a colleague or two who share their convictions. More often, they have to seek out teachers in other schools and districts to share their successes and failures, their victories and defeats. They find their associates through support groups, and through whole language newsletters and other publications.

What makes a whole language teacher?

Commitment

Becoming a whole language teacher is a bold decision for many. Once the decision has been made that being a professional means accepting responsibility for using the best available knowledge to educate every learner to the fullest extent possible, then prescriptive teaching material is out. The welfare of children cannot be left to authors of basals and standardized tests. The methods or materials that are inconsistent with the teacher's best professional judgment must go.

For some, this bold decision comes even before the first teaching, job, as a knowledge of whole language and a belief base is formed at the university. These teachers only have to learn how to do it, in the reality of a real classroom. For others the decision comes later, brought about by reading, by an in-service workshop, or by interaction with colleagues. They come to realize that they've been satisfied to accept limited success as the fault of pupils rather than of wrong methods, materials, exercises, and basals.

Some teachers come to realize that they've been whole language teachers for years — a liberating discovery! They are justified in their professional judgments. It's relatively easy for them to give up the things they've been doing, things they never really believed in, and to expand on what they always, in their hearts, knew was right. As they connect theory with practice, they put heart and head together and are greatly strengthened in their teaching.

Transition

For many teachers, the transition is pretty scary. They become whole language teachers quietly, step by step, ruffling as few feathers as possible and easing themselves and their pupils into it. The teacher's own style, the degree of flexibility in the school, district requirements and mandates, the nature of the community and the school population, traditions in the school and community, and the courage (or brashness) of the teacher all play a role, making each transition unique.

Here is one possible sequence for a teacher to follow:

First, assess your program.

- Is your present program not helping your pupils to become literate?
- Would a move toward whole language be better for your kids?
- Are you reasonably satisfied with your reading and writing program but concerned about integrating language development with the rest of the curriculum?

Next, consider what you are already doing that is consistent with a whole language program.

- Do you use thematic units? Is your classroom a literate environment? Is it organized around flexible activity centers?
- Are your pupils involved in authentic speech and literacy events? Do they help plan their school experiences and engage in problem-solving?
- Do you use a wide range of materials and involve pupils in a range of language functions? Are the materials easily accessible to them? Is there a lot of functional reading and writing going on?
- Are parents informed of what you are doing? Do you involve them in their children's education, in school and at home?

Then consider what you may be doing that is not consistent with whole language.

- Are you and your pupils controlled by basal readers, workbooks, text-books, and tests?
- Do you make the choices of what your pupils will read, what they will write about, how they will go about each task you assign?
- Are all your pupils doing the same assignments, the same work sheets, the same activities much of the time? Do you lecture a lot? Do your pupils seem always to wait for you to tell them what to do?

Finally, take the first steps toward whole language.

Make decisions

Decide which strong points to expand on and which negative ones to de-emphasize. Trust that small first steps will lead to other more important ones. Move your desk into a corner to support a shift away from a teacher-dominated room. Put materials on open shelves and ask the class to set rules for getting and using them. Rearrange the seating to facilitate pupil interaction.

Confront the basics

If your program is dominated by basals, workbooks, and tests, you will need to shift away from them to authentic reading. It can happen over time. A first step may be to ensure the availability of a range of materials. Arrange with school and/or public librarians to borrow a collection of appropriate books for your room. Get your kids involved in one or more paperback book clubs. Set up a store corner in your classroom and stock it with empty boxes and containers. Build your classroom, with the kids' help, into a literate environment.

Now cut back on your use of the basal, maybe one group at a time. Your top group can easily be shifted into a personalized reading program. If administrators or school policies require the use of basals, let the kids read through them quickly on their own, with occasional group discussions about particular selections. Then let the pupils choose their own material for sustained silent reading and develop book talks, dramatizations and other ways of sharing. Schedule individual conferences during the time you formerly met with the group.

Gradually move other pupils into a personalized, independent reading program. They'll need more support, no doubt, but you'll find they are more capable of independence than you expect, and are able to read sophisticated and complex material if it's interesting to them and they choose it. Liberating your better and average readers and helping them move ahead at their own pace has an added bonus: eventually their improvement will show on standardized tests and they'll raise the class mean score. Meanwhile, you'll have the deep-down satisfaction of knowing they did it your way. You'll know also what the tests don't show: they've improved their effectiveness, efficiency, and breadth of reading. And they enjoy reading!

Diminish the use of workbooks and exercise sheets for all your pupils. Save only the few exercises that might qualify as strategy lessons, those with whole, meaningful texts that might be relevant and interesting to your pupils. Begin to develop your own strategy lessons and ways of involving all your pupils in real literacy events — reading and writing for all kinds of purposes.

Begin developing strategy lessons for your least effective readers. The primary goal is to help them revalue themselves and the reading process. They need the most one-on-one support. They need meaningful, functional, relevant reading and writing experiences because they are the least able to deal with abstraction and because they become easily discouraged. Suitable strategy lessons will help them build the basic strategies of prediction, inference, self-monitoring, and self-correction. Gentle support and sensible materials suitable for their age and interests are what they need most of all.

Get rid of the Wombats

Virginia Ferguson, an Australian children's author and reading consultant, did a little study to find out how pupils recalled learning to read. She asked one pupil to read a book for her. "I can't. Miss. I'm only in Wombats." The Kookaburras had far greater confidence. It's clear to kids that being placed in a low group is stigmatizing, while being in a high group is an honor. Shifting toward more flexible cross-ability grouping is another way to shift toward whole language. Less able readers perk up when they realize they have much to contribute to group activities and group projects: a lot of information about some topics; ability to design and help produce displays and dioramas; a function in dramatizing stories. Insightful teachers find the strengths of all and encourage everyone to work in sharing ways.

Get writing going

Many teachers who shift to whole language find that their writing program develops most rapidly. Often that's because their pupils did very little writing before. Even young children can keep journals and write every day. Establishing a classroom mailbox for notes by and for kids makes writing an integral part of your program. Don't be too concerned that six-year-olds write anonymous nasty notes to each other. It isn't hard to redirect their energies into less anti-social functions.

It may be hard to let go of formal, textbook-based spelling and handwriting programs. But remember: misspellings are mostly confined to words being used for the first time, and punctuation is virtually impossible to teach anyway. Set yourself to watch and help pupils as they move toward conventional adult use. Keep folders of the writing kids produce and watch how their spelling and handwriting develop. Remind yourself, as well as administrators and parents, that invented spellings show development of personal rules, that lead, finally, toward standard spellings.

Most whole language teachers establish special status for writing that is published, and require editing to standardize spellings. In this editing for publication they build strategies for how to identify and correct non-standard spellings.

Children of all ages write best when they are able to choose their own topics. They don't need story starters or assigned topics. Within a thematic unit, by all means suggest a range of topics for choice, but also make it possible for kids to suggest a topic of their own.

The primary criterion for handwriting is legibility. The best way of helping children achieve greater legibility is making sure they care, because they have something to say to an audience they have chosen. Individual conferences enable you to offer support. Or you might meet with a small group of children you think can profit from help, to deal with particular aspects of handwriting still using their own writing as the base.

Set lines of communication

As you proceed, you will want to look at the lines of communication in your classroom. Neither you nor your pupils may be totally comfortable with a sudden transition to a classroom that encourages all kinds of discussions, deliberations, and other language transactions not solely through you. Maybe kids will mistake the shift for a lack of discipline, and chaos can be the immediate result. A gradual transition, and much talk with the kids about reasons and ground rules, will be wise. Here are some steps:

- Reorganize or re-establish "sharing" time so that the kids run it with rotating chairpersons. With the kids, establish rules for who speaks when, and how to ask questions or raise criticisms in courteous and supportive ways.
- Reorganize math and other instruction so pupils are working together, and encourage them to use discussion and interaction to solve problems.
- Create small groups with very specific group tasks. Make sure the participants know what they are expected to do and have some sense of how to organize themselves to do it.

Even older pupils may not have had any experience in these things. They will need careful support and guidance until they become comfortable with the changed ground rules. The key is to involve them in thinking through and setting up the rules. Like everything else worth doing in a whole language classroom, it may take time to reach the point where there is a maximum of functional language interaction, mostly on task.

Resolve the noise problem

Teachers have traditionally abhorred noise. Next to silence, it's the hardest thing to tolerate. We want to fill silence; we want to cut down on noise. Teach yourself to stand where you can see everything and observe what the noise is, who is producing it, and how it relates to what the kids are supposed to be doing. You'll often find that most of the noise is very much related to the kind of language transactions you want. When not, move in to help re-establish purpose. Who knows, confusion may reign because you took too much for granted and didn't anticipate problems kids would have in understanding what to do or in organizing themselves. Or you may have assumed more experience, interest, or background than was justified. That requires replanning, and then another shot at getting them on track. There is nothing wrong with reminding kids to keep noise levels down, but there's no profit in carping.

Maintain order

It's no harder to maintain order in a whole language classroom than in a teacher-dominated one. Kids involved in authentic speech and literacy events they helped to choose and plan will produce orderly activity. Whole language teachers do not abdicate control; they exercise it more subtly. The kids know who's in charge, and they know they can depend on the teacher when they need to. They know there is an order, a set of rules, and a structure in their classroom. Teachers plan for all this and keep watch constantly. But it isn't necessary to constantly assert authority or to constantly engage in battles with the kids for control. For starters, a well-organized whole language classroom eliminates the problem of kids who have to wait for the teacher to tell them what to do next.

There's always plenty to do, because the units are ongoing and because reading, writing, and discussing have their legitimate place.

Develop oral language

People learn how to converse, discuss, and listen by conversing, discussing, and listening. Kids who aren't very effective in any of these activities most likely haven't been involved in enough classroom speech events. Build a variety of ways of working in your classroom so that sometimes the kids work in twos or threes, sometimes in small groups, sometimes in larger groups, and sometimes together as a whole class. Legitimate activities will give kids opportunities to learn how to get their points across, how to plan what they want to say, what resources they need to have, and how to be understood and accepted in all kinds of interactions and presentations. Good kid-watchers monitor interactions and note how they can assist individual kids and groups in becoming more effective.

Plan

Long-range, middle-term and immediate plans should all be seen as opportunities for development toward long-term goals: expanding the pupils' language effectiveness, broadening their knowledge and conceptual base, and positively improving their attitudes toward themselves and others. Short-term plans that cover periods of days and weeks are unified by themes or units: solving real problems in science and social studies. They involve being sure that the right materials are available at the right time, reading a specific book to a group or to the class, organizing a trip to the post office to find out how the letters the kids have written to pen pals are processed. These are the ongoing activities that keep the medium and long-term plans moving. Whole language teachers also develop middle-range plans for individuals or groups: how to broaden the interests of a boy who only reads electronics catalogues, how to bring together a group of kids of mixed abilities who share an interest in computers.

Planning is a must. It means taking control back from the basal reader manuals, from the mastery-learning skill sequences, the workbooks and the test-makers. Professionals are always in control of their own work.

Whole language teachers have no choice. Other professionals may be able to advise you, but your plan must be yours and must involve your pupils' participation.

It's wise to document your planning. At all times you need to be able to show administrators where you've been, where you're going, and how everything you're doing relates to your plans. You need to be able to demonstrate that you don't need the manual to tell you what your kids need.

Evaluate for self-protection

Kid-watchers know the signs of growth, of learning, of teachable moments. Teachers know how to interpret what kids do, how to see the competence and the need that underlie what they do.

Keeping good records is part of being a good kid-watcher. Records are the stimulus to good planning, but also a matter of self-protection against unenlightened administrators who know only one way of evaluating students and teachers — standardized tests. Collect all kinds of evidence of the growth of your pupils: folders of the writing they produce over a year's time; tapes of each child reading; a series of anecdotes showing changes in work habits, in interests, in effectiveness; a record of what kids have read and how they've responded to it; photographs, videotapes, parent correspondence; analyses of performances on informal and formal tests. One of the most important kinds of evidence of the value of instruction is in the evaluations the kids are able to make of themselves. And nothing will get through to a skeptical parent like the satisfied voice of their child saying, "Now I can do it."

Form support and study groups

Whole language teaching is a grassroots movement among teachers. Deciding to take charge of your own classroom is an act of courage in an era of a shortage of jobs for teachers and a regressive back-to-basics curricular trend. It's particularly scary if you're the only teacher in your school to do so. Many teachers have formed support and study groups. They get together to cry on each other's shoulders, to engage in self-help group therapy, to share triumphs. They discuss whole language techniques, strategies, and units. They plan ways of dealing with skeptical colleagues, threatened administrators, bewildered parents. They find themselves engaged in in-service education for their colleagues, as well as for themselves. They organize presentations at conferences and plan their own public conferences and demonstrations. A loose network of such groups has developed. Some, but not all, call themselves TAWL, Teachers Applying Whole Language. Whole language newsletters are being produced. Conferences are being organized, including one in Halifax, Nova Scotia, that attracted 1500 delegates.

Bring the kids and the parents along

Whole language programs are sensible, but they seem strange to people used to traditional programs. Even kids may be expecting work organized around textbooks, workbooks, and sequenced exercises. Whole language teachers need to help pupils be aware of how they learn to read and write by reading and writing, of how they become better able to use language by getting lots of opportunities to use it. Have them keep folders of their written work over a span of time, a log of their reading, tapes of themselves reading orally every so often. They'll show themselves.

Take parents along with you. They appreciate hard-working teachers who respect their kids and who know what they're doing. Whole language involves a humanistic/scientific knowledge base, but there are no great mysteries in it. Parents can grasp the key notions. You're celebrating the language and language learning ability of their sons and daughters. You're helping their children grow while accepting who and what they are. You're treating them, their language, and their life experiences as inseparable wholes. Parents will appreciate with you a delightful invented spelling, a marvelous reading miscue, an ingenious punctuation strategy, just as they will appreciate the first sensitive attempt at poetry, a touching telling of the death of a pet, and the class-composed operatic representation of Tomie De Paola's book, *Strega Nona*.

Hold meetings with parents to explain your views of language, of learning, of teaching, and of curriculum. Suggest ways they can help and can judge their children's progress. With some support, parents can become enlightened kid-watchers too. They should be invited to visit the classroom often. When they come, help them understand what is happening and why. Parents will respond positively if they feel that teachers are professionals who really know what they are doing and genuinely care about their kids.

Don't apologize for deserting the basals and the spellers, but be prepared to help parents understand that you have better ways of helping their children develop and grow. They will become your greatest supporters and your best defense if you keep them informed and ask for their help.

Keep administrators on your side

Administrators, too, are an embattled lot these days. Many have become ardent supporters and implementers of whole language programs. However, many others are not well informed about language education, although they appreciate teachers who know what they are doing, who have strong commitments to their beliefs and to kids, and who are willing to take responsibility for their success or failure. Whole language teachers will need to make their plans available for review, to keep good records of activities and achievements, and to find opportunities to explain what they are doing and why they are doing it. Wise administrators will rely on effective whole language teachers to support the program and to bring it and the rest of the staff along.

Many whole language teachers involve their principals in their programs. They invite them to come in regularly to read to a group of kids. They encourage pupils to write notes to the principal that he or she will respond to. They share parent communications with the principal and make sure he or she knows when the class is doing something interesting and exciting. They encourage children to let the principal hear their reading, see their writing, and appreciate their successes.

Remind yourself and others what it's all about

One very important point for decision-makers, teacher educators, administrators, parents, and teachers themselves to remember is this: all kids are whole language learners, but there are no whole language classrooms without whole language teachers.

AFTERWORD:
WHOLE LANGUAGE AND THE
PEDAGOGY OF THE ABSURD

The success of whole language in changing the nature of education, particularly literacy education, makes it a highly visible target for political forces seeking to roll back educational change and shift education from a societal responsibility to a parental one. "It's the tall poppies that get cut down" say my Aussie friends and whole language has become a tall poppy, indeed.

Here are some comments that I made at an NCTE conference in 1991 which have proven to be prophetic:

In my workshops on whole language and in critical articles in journals people keep looking for the secret of whole language: a two word definition or a simple set of materials to plug into a conventional curriculum.

What whole language really is: Self-empowered teachers taking the best available knowledge about language, about learners, about curriculum, about teaching and about building the learning community and turning it into reality for learners in their classrooms. It involves a body of knowledge, and a humanistic philosophy that values all learners, but it is teachers who have proclaimed themselves professionals and who have turned this all into practical reality.

If you want to understand whole language you must, more than anything understand this new professionalism among teachers.

So I thought with all due respect for Eve Merriam's text that I would begin with a variation on her parable of the Wise Woman. (In Merriam's story
"The Wise Woman," neighbors are hunting for the secret to her wisdom.)

Once there was a strange secret gathering. It was composed of a
number of quite disparate groups. They had come together to try to
understand a strange and powerful force which was sweeping the land:
they knew it was powerful because it was shaking the foundations of
the most important educational institutions in the country: the textbook
publishers and the test makers. It was spreading from classroom to classroom, from school to school, from district to district, from state to state.
Teachers infected by the force were exhibiting strange changes of behavior and students were engaged in really abnormal behavior: they were
reading, they were writing, they were solving problems, they were asking
real questions and finding their own answers.

A group of experimental researchers were the first to offer their ex-
planations at the meeting: They had done careful meta-analyses of all
the important research (that is experimental research) and had reached
the unquestionably research-based conclusion that none of this could be
taking place. What teachers were teaching and what learners were learning had been shown by their research to be impossible. Furthermore,
said the researchers, they were outraged at the increasing frequency with
which teachers were telling them that they, the mighty researchers, were
irrelevant. They therefore concluded that these teachers are being de-
luded by evangelical gurus.

Then spake the publishers. They told tales of great upheaval: of nervous sales representatives carrying tales back from the field of teachers
demanding real literature in reading text books, of refusing to use work
books, of insisting on using money usually reserved for text book pur-
chase to buy real literature for their pupils to read. The publishers had
decided, they said, on a two tier response: they would capitalize on the
temporary fad of using real literature which had increased the sales of
kids' trade books by 500% in the previous ten years. Meanwhile they
would embark on a campaign of disinformation. All their subsequent
basals would henceforth be labeled whole language basals; thus they
would fool the teachers into thinking that they were part of the whole

language movement when they were not. Though it was too early to evaluate this strategy, reports from the field were mixed. A surprising number of teachers, it was reported, appeared able to detect phony whole language materials.

Then the school administrators spoke. The new force was becoming increasingly troublesome. There was no telling where it might break out next. It was even spreading to private and religious schools. Outbreaks had been noticed in the bible belt, in rural schools- even in the suburbs. In its worst form it disrupted usual power relationships. Teachers were being emboldened to take power- they were even taking the notion of site based management seriously and demanding real power in their classes. Even worse there were frequent reports of infiltration into the ranks of administrators. As this was uttered the administrators began to eye each other strangely. We've issued mandates, said the administrators, but we're not sure we'll be able to enforce them.

Now it was the politicians turn: There they were, governors of the states led by a former member of their group, who it was reported sat at the right hand, of the President. Not to worry they said. You folks are taking teachers far too seriously. We, politicians, have studied the educational scene in America- and we have found it to be a total failure. And we know why it has failed: the teachers and the pupils are to blame. We can solve that through a narrow national curriculum, a national test for teachers to weed out the trouble makers (and minorities) and a new test for kids. Leave it to us to leave no child, teacher or school untouched.

Writing anti-whole language into law

Strangely the greatest recognition of the soundness of whole language views of literacy and literacy education is that the so-called reading wars have been framed in the press and the speech and acts of politicians as for and against whole language. In the " ReadingWars" direct instruction of phonics and phonemic awareness are presented as research based (because they are not whole language) and the major premises of whole language are rejected as unproven or disproved though the evidence cited to support that claim does not examine any of the premises of whole language.

There have always been different views of literacy and literacy education. And of course these views do not separate easily into two mutually exclusive views. But a sustained campaign framed as for and against whole language has had two goals. One is to present a single narrow view of reading based on direct instruction of phonics as the scientifically proven alternative to whole language. And the other is to characterize anything other than this narrow approach as whole language in disguise. By doing so, not only is whole language marginalized but so is the wide range of alternate views in theory and research in the field of literacy.

To seal the victory over whole language of anti-whole language it was written into law, first in the Reading Excellence Act and then Into the No Child Left Behind revision of the Elementary and Secondary Education Act.

I've argued in other works, *In Defense of Good Teaching* and *Saving Our Schools,* that the real purpose of the attacks on whole language is to discredit public education and marginalize scientific views while replacing them with pseudo science. In the political climate of the early 21st century, as the Union of Concerned Scientists has argued, science is being shaped to serve the political agenda of the power elite.

The NCLB law serves the political agenda: each major principle of whole language is explicitly rejected and an opposite view is given legal status.

Differences in definitions of reading

In whole language reading is construction of meaning during a transaction between the reader and the text. It is making sense of print. The federal law defines reading as rapid accurate, automatic word recognition, with meaning the by-product. While we might agree that ultimately the reader must comprehend, what comprehension is, how it is to be achieved and judged are very different.

Those different definitions lead to different views of what learning to read is and how best to help children learn to read. They lead to very different research. The law draws on a summary of reading research by the National Reading Panel that excluded any research that was not an instructional experiment designed to teach phonics and word attack.

Whole language relies on a wide range of research on the reading process, reading development and reading instruction. Research methods from several foundational disciplines: linguistics, anthropology, sociology, developmental psychology, and education among others.

And the two views lead to very different evaluation. Whole language relies, to a great extent, on self evaluation by learners and kid watching by teachers. Tests like the Dibels, which judges reading by how many nonsense syllables a kindergarten or first grade child can sound out in one minute, are mandated in the enforcement of the law and used to classify beginners as at risk and failing.

Differences in theories of learning
In whole language, language is both a personal and social invention: human beings have the unique ability to think symbolically and to invent language both individually and socially. In this view written language is learned and develops in much the same way as oral language in the context of its functional use. The law takes the view that all learning is a response to direct instruction and there is little difference between how language is learned and how any skill is acquired. So materials for reading instruction are decodable built carefully only on skills taught out of context and sequentially. It rejects the whole language belief that learning needs to involve complete meaningful texts. In whole language, texts used in reading instruction are authentic and predictable for the learners.

Different views of teachers and teaching
Whole language treats teachers as knowledgeable professionals who know language, learning and children and know how to support literacy development building on what children know. In this view teachers are educated not trained. They are professionals who shape the instruction to fit the learners.

The law takes the direct instruction view that teachers are technicians who need to be required to teach a prescribed, mandated and scripted sequence of skills and need to be monitored to assure that they do so. In this view teachers are trained and highly controlled. They are not permitted to deviate from the precise sequence of the program. The law provides for paradigm police who make sure teachers don't deviate from the scripted programs.

Different views of curriculum

Whole language puts the focus in curriculum on starting where the learners are. The curriculum builds on the language, experience, interests and culture of the learners. The curriculum is based on problem solving and inquiry. While social objectives are important, personal objectives are also important so the curriculum is flexible to suit the characteristics of the learners.

In this view, pupils learn to read in the course of reading to learn and to enjoy literature.

Federal law says materials, methods, and objectives must be standardized and highly sequenced. The curriculum is the same for all regardless of differences in learners and progress is dependent on mastery of each set of skills before progress to the next. In this view, learners learn to read before they read to learn..

The future of whole language

In the history of the world there have been many attempts to label new theories and understandings as unacceptable, illegal and even sacrilegious. But Copernicus and Galileo's view of the universe eventually triumphed over church and governmental rejection. Flat-earth views had to yield as evidence accumulated that the earth is a sphere. Evolution became accepted even though laws were written to ban teaching it.

And in the future wise men and women will look back on this period in education as that of the pedagogy of the absurd in which invalid and unworkable methods and materials were the law of the land and sound and sane pedagogy was forbidden.

In North America and in many parts of the world, whole language is surviving in the classrooms of committed, professional teachers who know what they are doing in their teaching and why it benefits their students. The laws banning whole language and mandating anti-whole language promise an absurd level of success they can not possibly achieve while they turn classrooms into dismal unpleasant places in sharp contrast to the excitement and involvement in learning seen in whole language classrooms. Furthermore the penalties NCLB imposes on students, schools and school districts will produce a back lash among parents and state and local decision makers which will cause them to reject the law's mandates and turn back to the sane and sound alternatives.

Whether the term whole language survives as the term for what the movement has brought to education or not is not really important. Education which is optimally successful with the full range of learners in all societies will ultimately require professional teachers, who respect and are respected by their pupils. Whatever we call successful teaching in the future, it will depend on the knowledge teachers have of how language processes work and are learned and how language is at the center of human thought, learning and communication.